MEDITATIONS
ON MODERN
POLITICAL THOUGHT

MEDITATIONS ON MODERN POLITICAL THOUGHT

Masculine/Feminine Themes from Luther to Arendt

Jean Bethke Elshtain

THE PENNSYLVANIA STATE UNIVERSITY PRESS
University Park, Pennsylvania

First published in 1986 by Praeger Publishers.

Published in 1992 by The Pennsylvania State University Press, Barbara
Building, Suite C, 820 North University Drive, University Park, PA 16802.

Library of Congress Cataloging-in-Publication Data

Elshtain, Jean Bethke, 1941–
    Meditations on modern political thought : masculine/feminine
themes from Luther to Arendt / Jean Bethke Elshtain.

                  p.   cm.
    Originally published: New York : Praeger, 1986, in series: Women
and politics.
    Includes bibliographical references and index.
    ISBN 0-271-00864-4 (alk. paper)
    1. Political psychology.   2. Femininity (Psychology)
3. Masculinity (Psychology)   I. Title.
[JA74.5.E46   1992]
320′.01′9—dc20   91–46357
                                                  CIP

For Errol

Contents

Preface:
On Writing This Text

Sometimes books fall through the cracks. Such was the original fate of this modest work of political and theoretical interpretation. Written originally as part of a "Women and Politics" series published by Praeger and coedited by Ruth Mandel, director of the Center for American Women and Politics, Rutgers University, and Rita Mae Kelly, Center for Public Affairs, Arizona State University, *Meditations* did not so much disappear as fail to appear altogether. My fault in part. I was late delivering the manuscript, and when I turned it in at long last, Praeger was in the throes of pre-nuptial dealings with another publisher and my book was lost in the reorganizational shuffle. This is a common tale, alas. One just has to figure these are sometimes the breaks and to roll with the punches and other such comforting shibboleths.

I turned to other projects. But my regret that so few had had the opportunity to engage *Meditations* deepened. It seemed, and seems to me, a helpful volume for students of political thought—too complex to be merely introductory but modest enough in framework, approach, and execution to be accessible to all advanced students willing to do a bit of analytic and critical work. I hope this republication bears me out and that students and teachers find the book helpful.

The concerns which drove the writing of *Meditations* some six years ago remain vital and vivid. These revolve around the tension inherent in my position as a feminist political theorist who routinely challenges both feminism and political theory, forms of discourse indispensable to my work and lying at the core of my public and private, personal and political understandings and commitments. To constitute one's project in this manner is to be vexed in interesting ways.

One example must suffice. Perhaps it is best couched as a query: how is a thinker to defend her viewpoint, to urge her way of seeing as a compelling possibility for others, without launching her interpretive project from a standpoint of epistemological privilege— whether as a "woman" or a "feminist" or a "critical thinker"? There

ix

are feminist political theorists, cultural anthropologists, and liter-ary critics who make strong claims to privilege, insisting, as some do, that the vantage point "feminist" or "female" permits them to understand and to explain in ways not available in principle to either men or to anyone unsympathetic to the feminist project as they con-strue it. Refracted through feminist awareness and categories, this standpoint promises universal validity, superior insight (being a member of a subordinated class seems to be the key), and accounts that are somehow "holistic" and trustworthy. Men by definition can-not make such claims and women whose consciousness remains unraised are undermined by their "male blinkers," often exhibiting "male bias."[1]

Surely, however, our gender identities simultaneously *reveal* and *conceal*, and this holds for male and female interpreters alike. It is both plausible and likely that some modes of thinking and act-ing will be more accessible to a female analyst in specific circum-stances and in light of specific questions or problems than to a male analyst in those same circumstances given identical questions and problems. But the obverse also pertains.

I am reasonably certain that an eighteen-year-old American male has superior entrée into what it feels like to be a male teenager, opposed to war, yet compelled to register for the draft on pain of losing his federal student loan for college education than an eigh-teen-year-old female under no such compulsion. I am reasonably certain that I, as a middle-aged mother of four, have surer access to the world of mothering than a single male of my age and class. To turn to a textual example, I think I can offer a reading of Rousseau that keeps alive his ambivalence toward women and how this am-bivalence is variously represented. This interpretation, I would ar-gue, attuned as it is to Rousseau's paradoxes, comes closer to the "truth" of the perplexing Jean-Jacques than monotone, unidimen-sional representations of him as a simple misogynist, no more and no less. On such points of interpretation one must fight it out, draw-ing upon textual evidence to buttress one's claims.

Finally, of course, there is no finally—no ultimate and complete interpretation of any complex event, history, or text. Political dis-course is an open narrative, a conversation without closure. What a single theorist may reasonably provide is a way of seeing that pro-vokes and illumines, that incites the reader to his or her own reflec-tions. Sustaining discursive ambiguity is an enterprise bound to frustrate seekers after certainty. But students of nuance and culti-vators of skeptical commitment may find something of interest.

A few words are in order about who is likely to read this text and why it takes the shape it does. This book is not a textbook in any ordinary sense. I do not offer a survey of modern political thought. Although I do "round up the usual suspects" by the book's conclusion, I do not do so in chronological order. Thus both Machiavelli and Hobbes are discussed in the final chapter—after many who preceded them historically have been taken up. I include thinkers not usually found in the canon—Elizabeth Cady Stanton and Jane Addams, for example. Others are drawn in thematically, making appearances at different times. Students who require a more traditional treatment will be frustrated and are well advised to look elsewhere, for I chose the term "meditations" in my title advisedly. Meditations are acts of continued reflection on a theme or set of themes. To meditate is to muse, to dwell within that which one contemplates.

Every author writes with an audience in mind. If she is lucky, that audience is visible to her mind's eye from the start. If she is less fortunate, the audience may come into focus slowly or remain blurred and indistinct. Although the audience for this book was initially defined *for* me—this was to be a work in political theory aimed primarily at informed undergraduates—I continued to worry about tone, about being either too dense or too simple, about boring the already well-versed and confounding the untutored. I have a strong aversion to making any matter simpler than it is. Theory cannot be absorbed effortlessly through the pores of one's skin. But neither should an engagement with political theory turn into an ordeal, the stressful running of an abstract conceptual gauntlet. One should work at theoretical matters—but playfully. I hope this modest text creates ample space for work and play.

Many themes appear in the chapters below. These include individual and community, politics and war, reason and emotion, citizen and state. A thread that runs throughout is competing understandings of the "self," male and female. I proceed in part through interrogation, in part through exegesis, in part through polemic and straightforward exposition, putting questions to thinkers and assessing answers to my queries.

Why begin with Martin Luther rather than Niccolo Machiavelli? In our secular age, Luther raises quizzical eyebrows and Machiavelli prompts knowing nods, being lodged securely as the progenitor of modern political inquiry. There are several reasons, the most important being that Luther is a key composer of the theme song of the human subject in the modern West. Both Luther and Machiavelli are men of the late fifteenth and early sixteenth centuries, of transitional epochs. If the one, Machiavelli, promotes an instrumental notion of the autonomy of politics severed from moral chastening, the other, Luther, is essential in the articulation of the ideal of an autonomous, self-interpreting subject. Luther's "freedom of the Christian" figures in the story of American culture more centrally than Machiavelli's cunning of the prince.

Following the theme of the self, Immanuel Kant emerges as a salient force in the construction of liberal constitutionalism and its freely willing moral subject. Rousseau, surely, needs no justification in a book on modern political thought; nor should Hegel. Each makes robust contributions to our notion of the "self" in history and culture. As for Freud, we could not escape him if we tried. We are all marked by Freudian categories and we all (more or less) see the world through a Freudian lens. Freud has become our common sense and presents problems for our political understandings. Nineteenth-century feminist thinkers, most importantly Elizabeth Cady Stanton, make their appearance in Chapter 4. I pair Hegel and Jane Addams in Chapter 6, using each to illumine and highlight the other. Machiavelli and Hobbes turn up, at long last, in Chapter 8 as supporting players in a narrative of war and politics that features Hannah Arendt. Chapter 9 concludes by resisting conclusions.

Since *Meditations* first appeared in 1986 many things have changed or come into sharper focus. Although *Meditations* was not written with deconstruction in mind explicitly, I realized, upon rereading the text, that it steers a course between strong deconstructive and more straightforwardly critical and interpretive approaches. I am both skeptical and appreciative in my readings. I might add that I have no doubt, none at all, that there is a flesh-and-blood author behind the texts I take up as well as the one I have written. These authors, through their texts, are part of my intellectual landscape—a landscape that is not mine alone but that of all who participate in the velleities and contrarieties we call "Western culture."

Finally, the world has changed dramatically in the past few years. This new *Preface* is being written several days after President George Bush's dramatic announcement of major, unilateral cuts in nuclear preparedness and in the strategic deployment of the nuclear arsenal of the United States. This somewhat dates Chapter 8 of *Meditations* and I couldn't be more pleased. But Chapter 8 also, in its own modest way, gestured towards the remarkable democratic revolutions of 1989 and beyond. This, too, is a source of delight: Hannah Arendt was right when she insisted that hope is the root for political action and change.

                                                                October 1991

Note

1. Marilyn Strathern, a cultural anthropologist who is committed to the study of women in culture, provides a critique of such claims to privilege in an essay entitled "Culture in a Netbag: The Manufacture of a Subdiscipline in Anthropology" in *Man: The Journal of the Royal Anthropological Institute* 16 (Dec. 1981): 665–88.

Acknowledgments

For this reissuing of my book, my thanks go to Sanford G. Thatcher, Director, Penn State Press. Sandy was the editor on my first book, *Public Man, Private Woman: Women in Social and Political Thought* (Princeton, 1981). It is always good to work with him.

I am grateful to Dean Jacque Voegeli of Vanderbilt University for his continuing encouragement and support.

My biggest debt of gratitude is to my students—at the University of Massachusetts, Amherst, where I spent fifteen years and now to my students at Vanderbilt University. I continue to work on and to try out many ideas and formulations that make their way into texts such as this one in lecture and discussion in courses in Modern Political Thought.

To my husband and children, always.

1

Introduction: On Reading This Text

The goal of writing is to keep a beleaguered line of understanding which has movement from breaking down and becoming a hole into which we sink decoratively to rest.

William Carlos Williams

To pick up and sustain a "beleaguered line of understanding" for this work, it is necessary for me to return briefly to a previous one.[1]

I ask the reader to imagine two contrasting images. The first one sees many early feminists of the "second wave" which began in the mid-1960s and continues to the present taking a look back in anger at Western political thought. Anticipating a record of males writing texts to justify their dominance and to shore-up the oppression of women, these early seekers were not disappointed. The few possible and partial exceptions (Book 5 of Plato's *The Republic*, an explicitly feminist text by John Stuart Mill) only served to confirm the rule.

Sometimes texts were scoured for anti-woman references. Thinkers found guilty as charged were consigned to the ignominy they presumably deserved.[2] Thus one assault on Rousseau treats him as a figure upon whom derision is appropriately heaped, his thought construed as the illogical ranting of an overrated misogynist.[3] Within this *rejectionist* mode, feminism and Western political thought were set implacably at odds. To participate in the one—feminism—one must repudiate the other—'the canon' (with those few exceptions). Such was the aura of the early 1970s.

1

But Rousseau stubbornly refused to die. Nor did Aristotle re-
cede into the theoretical shadows, despite a number of determined
scholarly assaults.[4]

Although the rejectionists who cut themselves off from political discourse and its distinctive concerns and subject matter were
by far more visible and widely read, a second and contrasting image came slowly into focus by the late 1970s. Academic political
theorists with feminist concerns taught and read routinely those
thinkers who comprised the rejectionist rogue's gallery. Uneasy
with the blanket condemnations of popular polemicizing; unwill-
ing to endorse one-dimensional readings; convinced that feminism
jettisoned too much in tossing the whole Western political tradition overboard, losing along the way rich conceptualizations of order, freedom, power, authority, community, legitimacy, civic identity, citizenship, and so on, such theorists decided instead to knock
on the door of the tradition and shout, "Let me in!"

Construing the problem as women's confinement to the family
and exclusion from politics in theory and practice, a new strategy
for coming to grips with Western political thought unfolded: *assimilationism*. To put things right, the theorist scooped women up
into the political net. How does this work? A theoretical assimilationist might, for example, argue that Rousseau was muddled, un-
convincing, and inconsistent in locating women outside politics.
An unmuddled and more consistent Rousseau would acknowledge
that women, too, must be civic beings given many of his own
premises. Thus the assimilationist promotes feminist ends in the
present by bringing Rousseau's project to theoretical completion,
something Rousseau, presumably, would have done himself had
he not been mired in psychological and cultural misogyny.[5]

Serious theoretical engagements with Western political
thought emerged from readings dominated by such preoccupations. Fascinatingly, assimilationists and rejectionists offer a mirror image of one another. For the assimilationist 'purifies' past
thought, rubbing off all the unseemly protuberances, throwing out
the indigestible bits. This strategy is, of course, practiced by many
theorists with no interest in feminism, including the Soviet scholar
who, provoked by my reading of a paper on Rousseau at an international meeting in Moscow, proclaimed in a heated intervention:
"Why do you bother with Rousseau? Whatever is worthwhile,
Marx has incorporated!"

My reservations concerning feminist assimilationism are part
of a more general suspicion of all drives to synthesize. Too often
the only way we can assimilate a thinker, or make a theorist to

whom we are indebted fit with our own commitments, is by stripping him of his disturbing (by our lights) features; bleaching out
conflicts internal to his thought; thereby muting ruptures between
past and present. The assimilationist labors under an interpretive
imprimatur inseparable from her stated political obligation: to put
things right one must make them fit. Differences give way to constructed unities and that which is unreconstructable gets shoved
underground.

These criticisms intimate an alternative strategy, a mode of engagement with the past as embodied in particular texts that holds
in fruitful tension the disparities between our and earlier understandings. For a great divide separates Luther for whom saving a
human soul is a good for which he would forfeit his life, from a Mill
who tosses all pre-modern understandings into a conceptual bin
capitalized for rhetoric effect and labelled Instinct, or that which
is not Reason. More our contemporary, at least in the matter of
soul-saving, than Luther, Mill nevertheless inhabits a world certain
of its liberal beliefs, devoted to Progress and convinced of its forward march. To many disillusioned moderns, Mill's faith in Reason is as absurd as Luther's belief in the eternal soul, the resurrection of the dead, and the reality of angels was to Mill. Indeed,
Luther emerges as our peer in many ways for he lived in an epoch
of great dislocations and fears when the old was dying and the new
not yet born.

To see ourselves through Luther's eyes (or those of any thinker
who inhabits a world distant from our own) and Luther through
our own; to attempt to enter his world empathically, knowing one
cannot leap-frog out of history; to emerge from this encounter with
enhanced appreciation of disparities and a perhaps surprised recognition of commonalities, is a theoretical strategy that turns on a series of epistemological, historical, and linguistic queries. We en-
quire, for example, into the terms of production of a historic text
and the very different world in which *we* read and evaluate it.
What commitments and presuppositions prompt and help to form
our reading of a past text? What does it mean to say one 'understands' a text from the sixteenth century, or any other, thus-and-
so? We confront an interpretive dilemma central to the 'human
sciences.' Each successive era reads previous meanings in light of
its own field of meaning. We unavoidably confront dense layerings
of interpretation to which we add our own, refurbishing the discursive patina through our imaginative engagement with many
represented past(s).

My aim in this volume has not been to overcome conflict nor

to smooth over the rough edges of difference but to promote the enlivening cacaphony that results when one attempts to listen to many voices speaking different "languages."[6] Premature reconciliation between and among competing points of view closes off debate and stills distinctive voices. Theory should make the world more complex: "Nothing is as simple as one thinks"—or might like to think. And there is plenty to think about.

Notes

1. Jean Bethke Elshtain, *Public Man, Private Woman: Women in Social and Political Thought* (Princeton: Princeton University Press, 1981).

2. See, for example, the anthology *Not in God's Image* (New York: Harper Torchbooks, 1973).

3. Eva Figes, *Patriarchal Attitudes* (Greenwich, Conn.: Fawcett, 1970).

4. I took Aristotle to task in no uncertain terms in an essay that dates from this era. See "Moral Woman/Immoral Man: The Public/Private Distinction and its Political Ramifications," *Politics and Society* 4 (1974):453–73. I am not now recanting what I said then; rather, I am situating my thinking in a context in which feelings ran high and determination to peg those "responsible" for the historic oppression of women was a first order theoretical and political priority.

5. This example of the assimilationist strategy is my own recasting of the interpretive strategy of assimilationism.

6. See Bernard Williams, "Conflicts over Values," in *Moral Luck* (Cambridge: Cambridge University Press, 1981), p. 72. Williams insists that the "need" to overcome conflict is not so much required by logic and rationality as by social and personal pressures in times of social dislocation.

2

Luther's Two Kingdoms and the Eclipse of the Female [*Mater Ecclesiae*]

> They threaten us with death. They would do better to threaten
> us with life.
>
> *Martin Luther*

What do we think about when the name "Martin Luther" is mentioned? My students are almost unanimously clear: Luther is the reformer who fought against an oppressive Church, venal churchmen, ignorant superstition, and for "freedom."[1] Mind you, Luther's freedom may not quite be *our* freedom, these same students concede, but one vital blow for what has become our freedom in the West. Luther is a ray of light piercing the darkness of the Dark Ages. Luther in some sense made possible Jefferson, the Declaration of Independence, and my right to read anything I want: so the story goes. Luther has had a good popular press. We are all, in some ways, dominated by this Whiggish philosophy of history, tied as it is to visions of progress, breaking out of restraints, unleashing unbounded human energy, enabling "science" to take over from "faith."

If Luther is *for* freedom, as the story goes, it would seem that his revolution also, at least over the long run, served what we call the 'interests' of women—perhaps despite Luther's own time-bound prejudices in the matter. To be sure, Luther has been located by a few feminist thinkers as one in a very large company of patriarchalists intent on keeping women down whatever else they intended. I think Luther is far more paradoxical and interesting than the popular image holds and far less the unambiguous patriarch than narrowly construed argumentation would have it.

5

A more richly interpretive critique, however, does not leave Luther unscathed. By broadening the grounds of interpretation and critique, I shall call another 'Luther' into being as a problematic rather than paradigmatic thinker.

Luther Sic

The popular view, as I sketched it above, is not all wrong. There is a version of Luther that emphasizes certain features of his thought and downplays others, reasonably locating him as a father of freedom. But what sort of freedom and to what ends? Here it is necessary to introduce one of the perennial problems of political life and thought: authority. To set the stage for the 'legitimation crisis' of Luther's epoch one must conjure up images of dislocation and unsettlement: the break-down or ungluing of the medieval synthesis, including feudal ties of reciprocity and the manorial system; a Europe emerging from the devastation of the Black Death; the waning power of the papacy vis-à-vis princes; the rise of trade, commerce, and a new mercantile class.

The majority of people were non-literate (a better term than "illiterate" which presumes literacy as a standard), their lives suffused with powerful visual images and revolving around shared sacred rituals. Although all men and women 'believed'—this is a world permeated with the great Christian story—some were believers in different ways, heretics and reform spiritualists alike.[2]

Johan Huizanga speaks of a world passing away, a world swept by waves of mysticism and occasional violence, extremes of piety and kindness as well as cruelty. All this is familiar—perhaps too familiar because we see it through eyes that divide the world, before we even begin to look, into 'religious' and 'secular', a division that makes no sense at all in Luther's time.[3] For religion in this God-drenched age was a force in itself, one not reducible to the terms of particular socio-economic configurations.

A different sense of time prevailed for those living in Luther's epoch. Time was not yet money, fragmented into units and assigned 'value'. (The term *value*, which we often apply to an individual's moral beliefs and guiding motivations, is drawn from market economics.) Holy Days, most commonly celebrations of the lives of saints, were numerous and the rhythm of the seasons was tied to the life of Jesus: Advent, Christmas, Lent, Easter, Ascension. It was an era of Carnivals and Fools. For example: a carnival season ran from St. Martin's Day (November 11) to Shrove Tuesday in February. Celebrations that have come down to us as Mardi Gras or Carnivale (if you live in Venice) invited rituals of reversal, the wearing of masks and taking on other *personae*. Sexuality, from all the evidence, was fairly loose. It was normal for a city to have "a bawdy house and a beer house," in Luther's words. "Society was both permissive and conventional," writes John Todd in his biography, *Luther: A Life*. "Perhaps a cliche may be valid— the reaction from self-indulgence found an outlet in pilgrimages and formal religious gestures of all kinds, sometimes hysterical."[4] There were no ID cards, no licenses, no citizen dossiers, no fingerprints: the individual had not yet become a bureaucratic object.

One dimension of the complex Luther reflects this 'freedom'. He was, for example, a hearty beer drinker. More importantly, he exhibits relative ease about matters regarding the body and what we rather antiseptically call its 'functions'. He is notorious for his vivid descriptions of his bowel problems. But, more than that and more interesting in terms of representations of sexual identity and the self, is his condemnation of attacks upon the female body by those he thrashed as pretentious "schoolmen, the monks, and such other" who (he has one 'Crotus' in mind) dared "to blaspheme God's creature through whom he was himself born. It would be tolerable if he were to find fault with the behavior of women, but to defile their creation and nature is most godless."[5] Luther also took the side of a young married woman who learned her husband was impotent after marriage but wanted children. Luther advised her to seek a divorce and, if her husband wouldn't grant one, to have intercourse with another man but to ascribe "the children to the putative father...."[6] From our lofty perch, one afforded by the widely shared view that the modern hu(man) is the measure of all things, analysts and laypersons alike persist in proclaiming a sharp fissure between the supposed unfree or less-free past of the medieval and early modern period and our own epoch. We celebrate ourselves as rational beings, free from superstition, free, too, from nature, the controllers of our individual and collective destinies. Yet systematic attempts to suppress female sexuality by channeling it into and through rigid norms deepened with the emergence of modern civilization. Luther, in what seems to us an unusually liberated view of the matter given *our* present-mindedness, is, in fact, well within the range of expressible opinion of his age, hence more flexible than many subsequent thinkers.

I noted a 'legitimation crisis' and described above the markers of a time fraught with upheaval. Enter, explicitly, the problem of authority. Luther emerges as radical in his views, penning a political theology that bears both liberating and baneful implications. In the next section, I explore the negative features of Luther's concept of *political* or secular authority. For the moment, however, I shall focus on those features of Luther's life and thought that figure prominently as signposts on the freedom trail.

Hannah Arendt writes that "the moment we begin to talk and think about authority, after all one of the central concepts of political thought, it is as though we were caught in a maze of obstructions, metaphors, and figures of speech in which everything can be taken and mistaken for something else, because we have no reality, either in history or in everday experience, to which we can unanimously appeal."[7] Arendt is correct about the maze in which we find ourselves when we turn to the elusive yet inescapable matter of authority, linked as it is to what counts as freedom *and* order in any age. In our own era, for example, those who think about authority almost unanimously appeal, or make reference to, a perceived displacement, debasement, or sublimination of authority in our time. The modern thinker who sets out to pin down or uncover authority does so from a stance that accepts a crisis of authority as a starting point. That crisis of authority enters into everyday discourse when some among us lament the breakdown of the authority of teachers or parents, or when increases in crime are seen as a disintegration of the authority of the law, hence an invitation to lawlessness.

Arendt provides a helpful marker for consideration of the crisis of authority in Luther's era by reminding us that the roots of *authority* and *power* lie in the Latin *auctoritas* and *potestas*, respectively, each bearing divergent meanings. Authority appeared originally in a context in which it was inseparable from legitimation or entitlement: the right to speak, the right to be heard. Those *in* authority were augmenting (*auctoritas* derives from the verb *augere*, to augment) the foundation of political order, hence participating in the freedom of politics or the freedom that politics makes possible. (*Potestas* or power, however, meant simply the ability to compel or to enforce obedience and was linked to violence.) Interestingly, our word "author," the creator or originator of a text, also derives from the same root as authority: authorial, authoritative, authoritarian, authorize are overlapping moments that set the horizon for these considerations.

It is Luther as *author* and his dramatic claims that the authorial self can interpret and understand Scripture on its own, if he, or she, is true to the *authority* of Holy Writ, who helps to unleash an interpreting and reading self that forms part of the backdrop to our notion of individual freedom. The Word in hand, the text before us, insisting upon our author-ity, the individual—if armed with Luther's prodigious scholarly and rhetorical gifts—could breach the "second wall" of "the Romanists," the doctrine that interpretation of Scripture belonged to no one save the pope.[8] "Therefore it is a wickedly invented fable. . .that the interpretation of Scripture or the confirmation of its interpretation belongs to the pope alone."[9] In his "Preface to the Revelation of Saint John," Luther writes: "About this book of the revelation of John, I leave everyone free to hold his own ideas, and would bind no man to my opinion or judgement; I say what I feel."[10] Pitting *his* interpretation, and the authority of Scripture itself (Luther having pierced its secrets) against the Church, whose emmissary, Cajetan, was in sympathy with critics of Church corruption but insisted the Church's authority—its authoritative teachings—must be upheld, Luther helped to harness the nascent social energies of his day, including the eruptive force of the vernacular.

In a brilliant discussion of translation that prefigures Wittgenstein's ordinary language philosophy, Luther indicated that he had translated the New Testament "to the best of my ability and according to my conscience. . . . No one is forbidden to do a better piece of work." Whatever his mistakes, however, he would "not suffer the Papists to be the judges" for he knew better than they "how much knowledge, work, reason and understanding is required in a good translator; they have never tried it. . . ."[11] For help in translating—in making a translation "clear and strong" if one wants to speak "German, not Latin or Greek"—one must be true to the linguistic field in which one is immersed, one must look to "daily use." "We must not, like these asses, ask the Latin letters how we are to speak German; but we must ask the mother in the home, the children on the street, the common man in the marketplace about this, and look them in the mouth to see how they speak, and afterwards do our translating. . . ."[12] He helped to inaugurate an explosion of 'words'—his own and others—vulgar, earthy, often angry.

But matters are never so simple. If *an* authoritative interpreter is denied, who then has the interpretive right or freedom? Luther's deed to us is fraught with ambivalence: not just everyone, not just anything goes—despite his apparent interpretive pluralism in the citations above. For authority remains—the authority of internal textual evidence. Nevertheless, his claims are dramatic: the Christian requires only the pure Word needing neither the structured social forms of institutional Christianity nor the vast intellectual edifice of medieval thought that reached through reason toward God.

Though Luther was no Occamist, he placed strong limitations on the ability of reason to attain or aspire to the heavenly through human capacities. With the scholastic doctors as his explicit target, Luther restricts and restrains philosophy. Aristotle gets put in his place, much diminished from his pinnacle in Aquinas's systematic theology. Yet something of the Arabic philosopher Averroes's doctrine of the "double-truth," found in Aquinas, is also at work for Luther, namely, the idea that what is true philosophically may not be 'the truth', may not be theologically pure. We would say that Luther insisted upon diverse discursive universes having their own rules and tests, with theology on a different plane from philosophy. God's Word, Luther argued, needs no elaborate justifications; moreover, God is radically unknowable through reason. We have intimations of God only through the workings of His grace, not our own minds.

Luther's renewed emphasis on the simple, decent, pure Christian life—certainly this is how it was perceived by many during his lifetime and has come down to us—offers the promise of a democratic epistemology of simple faith against the aristocratic epistemology of Church scholars.[13] *Sola fides, scriptura sola*—faith alone, only the Scripture: the Christian had need of nothing more given the free gift of grace. The ground shifted from the ritual of the mass, turning on the special authority of the priestly office, to listening to the spoken word, the exhortations and interpretations from the minister to fellow believers. To *the* Word, Luther attributed great power. In one of his Wittenberg Sermons, 1522, he told the faithful:

> . . .faith must come freely without compulsion. Take myself as an example. I opposed Indulgences and all the Papists, but never with force. I simply taught, preached, and wrote God's word; otherwise I did nothing. And while I slept, or drank Wittenberg beer with my friends Philip [Melanchthon] and [Nicholas von] Amsdorf, the Word so greatly weakened the Papacy that no prince or emperor ever inflicted such losses upon it. I did nothing; the Word did everything. Had I desired to foment trouble, I could have brought great bloodshed upon Germany; indeed, I could have started such a game that even the emperor would not have been safe. But what would it have been? Mere fool's play. I did nothing; I let the Word do its work.[14]

This sounds rather disingenuous yet Luther clearly believed he was but an imperfect vehicle through which the awesome force of *the* Word worked its way.

What of women and the authorial self, women and the power of words if not *the* Word?[15] Luther does not address himself explicitly to this issue. Remember, he does call for the translator to use ordinary language, to consult "the woman in the house" as an expert on language. This is boldly populist and *that* may be problematic where women authors are concerned. Here I shall pose a paradoxical possibility for provocative purposes: Luther's deflation of the aristocratic epistemology of medieval philosophy and literature may have eroded rather than strengthened the authorship of women as well as the churchmen who were his explicit nemeses. For there were medieval women writers, not just a few rare women here and there but a respectable company whose work has come down to us. Writes Katharine M. Wilson, editor of a recent collection of the writings of medieval women: "In contrast with women writers of the more recent past, medieval women writers did not use male pseudonyms but identified themselves by name and sex. In addition, unlike the works of women writers of the seventeenth, eighteenth, and even nineteenth centuries, those of medieval women provide little evidence that they were ridiculed for or prevented from accomplishing their literary endeavors."[16]

Why didn't the medieval woman writer resort to the strategic ruse of the *nom de plume*? What happened between the fifteenth and seventeenth centuries that altered the social terms under which women authored, had author-ity with words? I shall hazard one point of interpretation that implicates Luther in the eclipse of female written authority: women are importantly privatized in Luther's thought. Women are not a special target: the overall effect of Luther's *political* theology is to strip individuals of social imbeddedness and a civic identity. Luther's doctrine of "the two Kingdoms" (discussed below) bifurcated the self: a radical interiority was invited, a privatization followed.[17] No longer situated in a social order with blurred boundaries between state and society, public and private, as we know them, the post-medieval women could go public only if she were not 'named', for the private realm was dictated as her sphere.[18]

I seem to have moved prematurely to 'Luther *non*', but it is impossible to interpret Luther unambivalently: his work is so fraught with tensions and lurchings that, to be true to his complexity, one cannot endorse the Luther of Whiggish history. Take, for example, Luther on the family and the woman in the home. We find a powerful insistence on conjugal equality, though 'man' and 'wife' have different authoritative statuses as men were heads of households. Men and women are bound by the same set of moral rules and each has available a life of simple piety, each can know "the freedom of the Christian." The social relations of everyday life gained a new sanctity, no longer being construed as second best to lives of the ecclesiastical orders. The "natural desire of sex" is compatible with mutual respect and is granted new legitimacy.[19]

An enrichment in intimate life, including more open expression of familial love and devotion, is attributable in part to the revolution in sensibility Luther helped to inaugurate. This transformation is marked in a poignant letter to his son. Luther addresses "Hans Luther" as "dear little son" and signs "Your loving father." He writes his child a vivid tale of a beautiful garden where "many children are," wearing "golden jackets" and gathering "nice apples under the trees," riding "pretty little ponies with golden reins and silver saddles." The point of the tale—a picture of heaven for a child—is to instruct the child in righteousness but also to take some of the sting off an always present possibility in an era when child mortality indexes were, by our standards, breathtakingly high. Luther is preparing his own "dear little Hans" for the garden.[20]

It is a moving letter so dramatically at odds with Luther the thundering polemicist one wonders: can it have been written by the "same" man? The answer is "probably not," for Luther displays a many-sidedness that strikes us as peculiarly modern. His is at one and the same time a self-certain self proclaiming at the Diet of Worms: "I neither can nor will revoke anything, for it is neither safe nor honest to act against one's conscience," and a self that peers over the abyss and sees. . .nothing: "Ich bin's nit."[21] In our moments of self-conscious acknowledgement of the demands and authority of a free conscience, even if there be risk, and in our moments of existential dread, we recognize Luther as one of us— male and female alike.

Luther Non

Sheldon Wolin, in his interpretation of Luther in *Politics and Vision*, sees Luther attempting to depoliticize religious thought by assaulting the ecclesiastical polity—a complex *ordo,* or order, in which *regnum* and *sacerdotium* comprised aspects or moments within a greater whole, the *respublica Christiana*.[22] Yet, argues Wolin, Luther's "depoliticized religious thought" exerted and continues to exert a profound influence on political structures and ideas. W. D. J. Cargill Thompson, on the other hand, in an essay, "Martin Luther and the 'Two Kingdoms'," depicts Luther as a "political theologian" whose doctrine of the Two Kingdoms (*die zwei Reich*) set forth a theory of temporal government with serious consequences.[23] The difference between these positions is not great for each concurs on the most important point: that Luther is aptly located within the domain of political theory.

Interestingly, it is with Luther's explicit understanding of temporal authority that the picture of Luther the freedom fighter is most out of focus. Within his vision of the necessity for and justification of the secular arm, we see a harshness that inclines toward political authoritarianism, toward absolute rule. The markers of the story recur back to the question of authority, inseparable from issues of legitimacy, force, order, as well as freedom. In "An Open Letter to the German Nobility," Luther appeals to the secular princes to reform the Church by revolting openly against its institutional forms and the authority internal to, and flowing from, those forms. His treatise is a wide-ranging, frequently vituperative rejection of the ecclesiastical edifice of medieval Christiandom. He strips the Church, as an institutional edifice, of authority—he deauthorizes the Church—yet he simultaneously celebrates secular authority.

The paradox here requires no hermeneutical cleverness to expose. In depoliticizing the Church, Luther does not so much break the bonds of authority as draw them tighter by providing for the flow of *all* legitimate authority over persons and events, over 'externals', to secular rule. Assaulting the "three walls of the Romanists" (I discussed the "second wall," the pope's exclusive interpretive authority above) Luther counters the claim that temporal power has no jurisdiction over the spiritual. To the contrary, the pope should have no authority over the emperor or any other lawfully established princes. But the obverse does not pertain. "I say," he writes, that "the temporal power is ordained of God to punish evil-doers and to protect them that do well...therefore [it should] be left free to perform its office without hindrance throughout the whole body of Christendom....[24] The nobility must set themselves against the pope "as against a common enemy." Further deauthorization of the Church is proclaimed by Luther in another of his great treatises, "The Babylonian Captivity of the Church," in which he takes on the sacraments and diminishes the Church's mission as dispenser of sacred ritual.[25]

By stripping political power of possible restraints exercised by ecclesiastical institutions, and by downgrading the "right of resistance," a major strain in medieval thought lodged in the idea of a social contract, Luther squeezed out space for notions of rule based

on the consent of the governed. Luther limits resistance to that of
an individual commanded in a matter of faith, but faith, like freedom, pertains only to the "inner" self, not to "externals."[26] In
general, the prince should be obstructed in his grim work neither
by pope above nor the people below. A new theory of the state and
an attack against the doctrine of a natural right to resist tyranni-
cal rule go hand-in-hand in Luther's thought. Luther's symbol of
temporal rule is the sword—the bloody sword always unsheathed
and at the ready.

True Christians—and they are few—have no need of any institutional edifice. But the vast majority require reproof and cor-
rection: for this Luther turns to the secular arm, interweaving
church and state into one edifice of power that becomes the *Lan-
deskirche*, the state church. Given Luther's bias against institutions, combined with his greatest fear—disorder, chaos—he is
forced to rely on secular authority, indeed to depend upon it, up-
holding only the weak reed of the prince's conscience as a check
on his own power.

Luther's celebrated 'priesthood of all believers' and freedom of
the Christian, when translated by others into directly political
terms, brings into painful focus a "Luther" repressed in the traditional account I noted at the beginning of this discussion. Remember: Luther hated and feared disorder, insisting it must be put
down at all costs. Temporal government must have the power to
suppress disobedience with no interference from institutional
church authority. The kingdom of this earth is primarily the kingdom of evil-doers and they must be restrained. Politically disturbing features of his views emerge with searing clarity in the famous
case of the Peasant Revolt.[27] Luther's response demonstrates that
when the chips were down, he could turn nowhere but to the
prince and call upon him to slay without mercy those who had
dared to take up arms under Lutherian slogans of the radical equality of all Christians—the priesthood of all believers.

Unfortunately, Luther seems to turn to force enthusiastically,
not reluctantly. The peasants, Luther cries, merit "death in body
and soul." They are "faithless, perjured, lying, disobedient knaves
and scoundrels" for reneging on their oath to be "true and faithful, submissive and obedient" to their rulers. The only result of
their foul actions is murder and bloodshed, turning "everything
upside down, like the greatest disaster." Given the threat posed by
the insurgents to law and order, "everyone who can" should
"smite, slay and stab, secretly or openly, remembering that nothing can be more poisonous, hurtful or devilish than a rebel."[28] It

is better that all the peasants be killed rather than sovereign authority destroyed. This is very strong stuff.

Luther wrote a follow-up pamphlet to explain the first, which had disturbed even his most faithful followers by its open blood-thirstiness. The crux of his second message is there is no avoiding the obligation to obey established civil authority. God is the author of the kingdom of the world and all who are not true Christians—nearly everybody save a few of authentic faith—belong to this kingdom alone. The world of fallen man is fundamentally orderless; hence, order must be imposed. Luther concludes on the grim note that the world cannot be "ruled without blood." The bloody sword is described as God's rod, a statement that cries out for a psychoanalytic gloss so obviously that it is best to demur. But it is hard not to concur with Ernst Troeltsch's harsh judgement: "Within the law of the State Luther's rigid idea of Original Sin and his demand for severe discipline, his contempt for the masses, and his conception of the civil authority as the representative of Divine punishment and reward, inclined him to extreme severity, and he was urgent in recommending the exercise of penalties like breaking on the wheel, decapitation, and torture."[29]

Luther additionally opens up the self to more far-reaching control by the temporal powers in his assault on the laxity of Church-inspired social forms—the festivals and holy days mentioned above. Luther would reduce the whole lot to Sundays only because feast-days, with Church sanction, "are now abused by drinking, gaming, idleness, and all manner of sins.... There are, indeed, some mad prelates who think they are doing a good work if they make a festival in honor of St. Ottilia or St. Barbara or some other saint...but they would be doing a far better work if they honored the saint by turning a saint's-day into a working-day."[30] At this juncture we are brought back to Luther's understanding of 'the self', or of that self that figures in his third foundational treatise, "The Freedom of a Christian." It is, to our way of thinking, both a familiar and a strange freedom. Familiar because we recognize its individualism and evocation of a kind of radical, interior subjectivity. Strange because we are not comfortable with paradox. Being the children of liberal society, it makes no sense for us to be told that the Christian is a perfectly free lord of all and subject to none yet, simultaneously, is a dutiful servant of all, subject to all.[31]

For Luther there is no contradiction. Just as there are two kingdoms, man has a twofold nature, the spiritual and the bodily, the inner and the outer. It is the inner man who is free and righteous and this inner man is justified by faith alone. He must obey

God's commandments first in his heart and soul—first and, it should be added, foremost. The true Christian needs neither the law, nor good works, nor institutions. Yet he is active in loving service to others even as he must be subject to governing authorities in externals. That is the story and it is one that quickly goes underground, becoming a tale of two selves: one who retreats into the citadel of inner freedom, accepts a sharp bifurcation between public and private morality and, in thus accepting, is drawn into the orbit of whatever power is dominant at the time. Troeltsch explains the impoverishment of Lutheran social theory, as compared with Catholic and Calvinist social thought, by the fact that Lutheran Christian individualism retired behind the line of battle of "all external events and outward activity," having no theory of a form for social life other than the state.[32]

My final reflections bear specifically on Luther and the eclipse of the female, of *mater ecclesiae* or Mother Church. The deconstruction of potent and authoritative female images often goes unmarked in received notions of Luther and the Protestant Reformation. But this matter is an intriguing one. The institution Luther aimed to strip of all authority was construed in gendered terms as female, specifically as a mother, *mater ecclesiae*. The Church as mother is evoked early on in patristic literature. The Church brings forth new life and nourishes all humanity at her breast. To be sure, this imagery is ambivalent for this 'mother' required and nurtured male mediations. Nevertheless, it *is* mother, not father, Church (also sometimes called "the bride of Christ") and its "care-taking" authority Luther assaults. This is the institutional moment of Luther's masculinization of theology.

In *Jesus as Mother: Studies in the Spirituality of the High Middle Ages*, Caroline Walker Bynum details a feminization of religious language in twelfth-century life. The markers of this feminized discourse included dramatic use by male writers (primarily members of the Cistercian order) of powerful female images to express their ambivalence about the exercise of earthly authority and to depict their relations to those over whom they held authority in maternal terms. Abbots and brothers are referred to as mothers. Devotion to the Virgin increased as did devotion to female saints, with the percentage of saints who were women undergoing a steady increase.[33] Bynum indicates that "there is some reason to hold that the increased use of marriage and motherhood as metaphors in the twelfth century reflects a more positive evaluation of these institutions in society . . . . Saints' lives begin to emphasize the influence of mothers on children at the moment when motherhood becomes an important image of God's activities." The locution "mother-Jesus" came to stand for compassion, nurturing, and union. Argues Bynum: "Throughout the Middle Ages, authors found it far easier than we seem to find it to apply characteristics stereotyped as male or female to the opposite sex."[34] If to this feminized discourse one adds the writings of thirteenth-century women mystics, discussed by Bynum, a rich picture of flourishing female-constituted spirituality emerges.

The symbolic-sacral moment of Luther's masculinized discourse lies, then, in his explicit diminution of the symbol of the Holy Mother and his repudiation of maternal tropes and metaphors more generally. *Salve Regina* chanted medievalists: Hail, Holy Queen. Hail—and farewell—Luther insists. "They put that noble child Mary right into the place of Christ," Luther laments. "They fashioned Christ into a judge and thus devised a tyrant for anguished consciences, so that all comfort and confidence was transferred from Christ to Mary, and then everyone turned from Christ to his particular Saint. Can anyone deny this?"[35] This is one of the chief sins of the Romanists: they would have us rely more on "Mary the Mother of Jesus, and the Saints," he insists, than on *the* Word.[36]

Why should this matter, especially to a desacralized age such as our own? Moreover, did not the veneration of the Mother 'oppress' women? Perhaps we have been too quick to leap to the conclusion that a theology without a dominant female symbol, whatever faults we may find with 'her' from our standpoint, and a social world bereft of the authority such symbols confer on women—I say symbols in the plural because the plethora of medieval female saints were also obliterated inside Protestantism—is a matter of little import to us. We tend to think in reductive ways, for example, when construing power in crudely binary terms: some have it, some don't, and those who do can compel those who do not. Thus we lose subtler yet no less powerful webs of meaning and significance.

Feminist-informed cultural anthropology offers a critical wedge into Luther's deconstruction of female religious authority and authorities. The rise of secular male dominance is a complex, many-faceted question. But the "symbolic mechanisms" that help to establish this dominance include the loss of guiding female symbols and the preeminence of male symbols.[37] The symbol of the succoring Mother, sacred yet not terrifying, available to all her children, existed in tension with the symbolism of women as the bringers of sin and the subsequent downfall of hu(man) kind. The

masculinization of theology in Protestantism, with veneration of
Mary condemned as ignorant idolatry, did not usher into some
glorious new day for women. Instead, it invited the loss of a female-
linked transcendent moment, a historic rupture we have yet to explore fully. The individual mother in the family may have gained
a new status, though this was already happening in the high middle ages, but the female—as metaphor, as politically charged symbol, as emotional repository of human hopes—faded. Luther decon-
structed, perhaps, more than he knew.

We are haunted by Luther—his overpersonalization of religion
and under-institutionalization of political and social life; his augmenting of secular authority and advocacy of civic passivity; his
severance of public and private morality. The darker side seems,
as this discussion ends, to prevail. But there is that other Luther—
not Luther the champion of freedom as we claim it—but Luther the
avatar of individual conscience, the gentle family man who pic-
tured golden gardens for a son, and grieved long for a dead daugh-
ter. This Luther is perhaps best exemplified in his nativity sermon
on "The Birth of Jesus," a tale, as Luther tells it, of the infusion
of ordinary events with extraordinary meaning, a homey, down-
to-earth story of the birth in humble surroundings of a Savior who
came among us as a vulnerable infant, "a true Baby, with flesh,
blood, hands and legs. . . ."[38] It is this Luther of simple piety,
shorn of thundering judgments, for the moment free from guile
and anger, who comes into view as well. Alas, in the genealogy of
modern political thought since Luther's death in 1545, this is not
the Luther who has prevailed.

Notes

1. Luther's life spans a number of tumultuous decades, made so in
part by his activities. Born in 1483, Luther died in 1546. His contemporary, Machiavelli (1469–1527), set the basis for subsequent theorizing
about politics and morality, or the necessary (in Machiavelli's view)
amorality of politics, in much the way Luther irrevocably altered our thinking about the human subject and the freedom of that subject. Machiavelli
is discussed in Chapter 8.

2. Those omitted by definition from the medieval synthesis, for example, Jews, nevertheless existed inside their own world of belief. There
were no "secularists" as we understand the term.

3. Johan Huizinga, *The Waning of the Middle Ages* (Garden City,
N.Y.: Doubleday Anchor Book, 1954).

4. John M. Todd, *Luther: A Life* (New York: Crossroad, 1982), p. 16.

5. Quoted from Jean Bethke Elshtain, *Public Man, Private Woman* (Princeton: Princeton University Press, 1981), p. 87.

6. Also cited in ibid., p. 88.

7. Hannah Arendt, *The Human Condition* (Chicago: University of Chicago Press, 1958), p. 136.

8. Martin Luther, *Three Treatises* (n.p.: Fortress Press, 1960), from "An Open Letter to the Christian Nobility" (3–114), pp. 20–23.

9. Ibid., p. 23.

10. "Preface to the Revelation of Saint John, 1522," in *Martin Luther*, ed. E. G. Rupp and Benjamin Drewery (London: Edward Arnold, 1970), p. 98.

11. "On Translating: An Open Letter, 1530," in Rupp and Drewery, *Martin Luther*, pp. 87–91, 87.

12. Ibid., p. 88.

13. See the discussion in Sheldon Wolin, *Politics and Vision* (Boston: Little, Brown, 1960), pp. 141–64, 152.

14. "Extracts from the Wittenberg Sermons, 1522," in Rupp and Drewery, *Martin Luther*, pp. 100–2, 102.

15. It would be unfair to criticize Luther for not putting women in the pulpit immediately contrary to all extant social arrangements and expectations. But posing the author-interpreter issue is reasonable—there were reading and writing women.

16. Katharine M. Wilson, ed., *Medieval Women Writers* (Athens, Ga.: University of Georgia Press, 1984), xix. See also Peter Dronke, ed., *Women Writers of the Middle Ages* (Cambridge: Cambridge University Press, 1984).

17. Obviously, Luther's work didn't bring about this result single-handedly. Complex social and economic transformations were also at work. The discursive background to Luther's emphases was set very early, for example, with St. Paul's insistence on freedom as part of an inward domain. See Hannah Arendt's discussion, "What is Freedom?," in *Between Past and Future* (New York: Penguin Books, 1968), 145.

18. There is an additional eclipse of symbolic and discursive representations of the female or the feminized in Luther's thought given his stripping of the greatest of all female symbols—Mary—of her sacral authority and role, together with his repudiation of the saints. I turn to this matter in greater detail below.

19. See a more complete critical dissection in Elshtain, *Public Man, Private Woman*, pp. 80–92.

20. "To Hans Luther at Wittgenberg, 19 June 1530," in Rupp and Drewery, *Martin Luther*, p. 153.

21. "Luther's Answer before the Emperor and the Diet of Worms, 18 April 1521," in Rupp and Drewery, *Martin Luther*, pp. 58–60, 60. Erik Erikson, in *Young Man Luther*, offers a dramatic account of the "fit in the choir" during which Luther fell to the floor crying, "Ich bin's nit" or "non sum" (New York: W. W. Norton, 1958), pp. 23–40.

22. Wolin, *Politics and Vision*, p. 143.

23. W. D. J. Cargill Thompson, "Martin Luther and the 'Two Kingdoms'," in *Political Ideas*, ed. David Thomson (New York: Penguin, 1982), pp. 34–52, 34, 40.

24. "Open Letter," in Luther, *Three Treatises*, p. 17.

25. "The Babylonian Captivity of the Church," in ibid., pp. 115–261.

26. See "Secular Authority: To what extent it should be obeyed," in Rupp and Drewery, *Martin Luther*, pp. 107–12.

27. "Revolt" in the singular is a bit of a misnomer for the reference is to not one but a series of uprisings in 1524–25 by peasants pressed by economic change and anxious to recover lost liberties.

28. "Against the Robbing and Murdering Hordes of Peasants, May 1525," in Rupp and Drewery, *Martin Luther*, pp. 121–26.

29. Ernst Troeltsch, *The Social Teachings of the Christian Churches*, vol. 2, trans. Olive Wyon (Chicago: University of Chicago Press, 1981), p. 533.

30. "Letter," in Luther, *Three Treatises*, p. 73.

31. "The Freedom of a Christian," in ibid., pp. 262–316.

32. Troeltsch, *The Social Teaching of the Christian Churches*, p. 540. The great Dietrich Bonhoeffer, who broke from the official state Lutheran Church over Nazism, found the Lutheran conception of Church and community impoverished compared with Catholic teaching. To express a "concrete solidarity" he turned, in part, to Catholic sources. See *The Cost of Discipleship* (New York: Macmillan, 1978).

33. Caroline Walker Bynum, *Jesus as Mother: Studies in the Spirituality of the High Middle Ages* (Berkeley: University of California Press, 1982), p. 137.

34. Ibid., pp. 142, 162.

35. Quoted in Todd, *Luther*, p. 319.

36. A feminist-informed interpretation of Mary may be found in Marina Warner, *Alone of All Her Sex: The Myth and Cult of the Virgin Mary* (New York: Vintage Books, 1983).

37. I am relying here on Peggy Reeves Sanday's fascinating study, *Female Power and Male Dominance* (Cambridge: Cambridge University Press, 1981).

38. Quoted from Hugh T. Kerr, ed., *Readings in Christian Thought* (New York: Abingdon Press, 1966), p. 157.

3

Kant and Rational Politics:
Woman as a Suspect Category

> We are therefore justified in saying that our thinking subject is
> not corporeal: in other words, that, inasmuch as it is represented
> by us as an object of inner sense, it cannot, in so far as it thinks,
> be an object of outer senses, that is, an appearance in space.
>
> *Immanuel Kant*

In her widely discussed book, *In a Different Voice*, Carol Gilligan links women's voices to a morality that locates responsibilities and conflicting duties to self and other within a dense social
network.[1] This is in contrast to the male voice which refracts
moral conflict through the prism of abstract right. These, at any
rate, are Gilligan's empirical observations as framed within the
scales of moral development and evaluation associated with
Lawrence Kohlberg's cognitive psychology. Kohlberg is famous for
his "six stages" of moral development, the sixth and apogee being that ultimate moral plateau whose occupants are distinguished by their ability to make moral judgments, and to reason
about moral conflicts, in light of and in line with universally valid
transhistorical stipulations of justice and right. (Justice and right
are posited as prior to and independent of any given social context
in this scheme of things.)

It turns out that men and boys when tested consistently come
closer to the highest stage and attain it than women and girls: this
is a Kohbergian constant. That Kohlberg based his scales of moral
reasoning on a study of 84 boys followed over several decades is
instructive. More interesting for this discussion, however, are the
specifically Kantian features of Kohlberg's psychological-moral
scales.[2] The Kantian influence is traceable through the work of the

great Swiss psychologist, Jean Piaget. Piaget's theory is avowedly Kantian in its tacit presumptions and explicit evaluations and it is Piagetian theory which Kohlberg, in turn, empiricized.

Thus when Gilligan insists that women tend to fall through the net of Kohlberg's moral web, turning up with lower scores than the men, she is making a claim, however muted, concerning the nature of Kantian rationalism and its possible gender-linked features. The strategy Gilligan, as a developmental psychologist, pursues is to resist Kohlberg's conclusion that fewer women attain the highest stage of moral thinking (for whatever reason). She questions Kohlberg's interpretation of his evidence, arguing that women's voice is different—not superior to the abstract male voice but authentic, valid, and worthy of recognition and consideration in its own right.[3]

This contemporary debate about moral reasoning and male/female differences invites us to retrace the emergence of the discourse Gilligan turns on its head in its current psychological form. Is there something in the *nature* of Kantian moral philosophy that *necessarily* locates woman as a suspect category from the point of view of Kant's rationalist project? To do even minimal justice to this matter in a single chapter requires that we set the stage by offering up the lineaments of Kant's systematic philosophy and its possible implications. The woman question, as it was called in the eighteenth century, gets folded in along the way at various points.[4]

Kant's Moral Philosophy and (Some of) Its Implications

The systematic philosophy of Immanuel Kant is one of the enduring monuments of the Enlightenment, that grand intellectual and cultural movement in eighteenth-century Europe and America marked by a celebration and defense of reason and 'science' against tradition and 'prejudice'. Kant did not understate what he believed to be his achievements, claiming for himself a 'Copernican revolution' in epistemology, ethics, and metaphysics. Revolutionary he may have been, but he emerged in a context that deeded to him a philosophic tradition rich in pitfalls and possibilities.

If, for example, one segues to Kant on the heels of an immersion in Luther, Kant seems strikingly familiar. His project offers a grand, systematic construction of Luther's split between the inner and the outer, repeating Luther's concentration on inner faith and purity of motive rather than 'externals'. Kant's strong vision of moral autonomy and the freedom of the self recalls Luther's "freedom of the Christian," although Kant grounds his freely willing self on a priori epistemological presumptions and Luther relies on the "soul." In Kant's world there are two realms: the "noumenal" realm of freedom and the "phenomenal" sphere of determinism and natural causality. Kant's self, like Luther's, is divided. The line of fault, Kant insists, severs a real and noumenal being "in itself" from those phenomenal and determined features of self that inhabit a realm of appearance, the world in which we appear before our fellow men and women. The freely willing self has no phenomenal form.

Kant's account requires that each person insofar as he is a "real, atemporal, noumenal self," free and autonomous by definition, represent himself as a thinking subject in *noncorporeal* or disembodied terms. The thinking self is not the embodied self but "sheer activity and therefore ageless, sexless, without qualities, and without a life story."[5] Reason "belongs to the inner sense only."[6] Other human beings, as phenomenal objects who are external to me, are "mere appearances." Kant's definition of reason severs knowledge and understanding from our particular histories as men or women *in* history, as beings who *have* a history.

The most important point for our consideration is Kant's contention that the self is divisible into noumenal and phenomenal aspects. The former is "independent of, and free from all . . . necessity" and "from all influence of sensibility"; the latter is bound up with nature, having an empirical character like other things in nature, and is known to others through the "powers and faculties he reveals in his actions."[7] Kant's free and rational self cannot initiate anything: "no action begins in this active being itself."[8] The lack of any compelling account of action poses a serious problem for Kant's philosophy from the standpoint of political theory. The nature of this problem is best explored by examining Kantian freedom further.

Kant's definitions of human freedom and autonomy flow from his initial presumptions concerning man's dual nature. But what is Kantian freedom? The role this concept plays in Kant's discourse is that of an a priori: a characterization of the metaphysical position of human beings as rational agents. Freedom's noumenal nature is such that one can never look to history or experience in order to assess contrasting ways of life as more or less free. Indeed, one cannot establish the criteria for such an assessment at all, for freedom in Kant's system has never been and will never be embodied in social forms—again the parallels to Luther are striking.

'Freedom' as a concept is wrenched from any application in the phenomenal realm; thus it plays no substantive role within Kant's understanding of persons as actors in public and private spheres. The implications for feminism, or any protest movement against the status quo, are serious for Kantian freedom cannot serve as a focal point for political struggle. Historically, freedom, like equality or justice, has been used either as a weapon to put pressure upon social practices and institutions with an eye to reforming them through politics, or deployed in a counter-rhetoric to shore up a given order. Kant's removal of freedom from its links to human history and experience eviscerates it as an evaluative term of political discourse involving concrete claims *within* social and historical reality.

This discussion is strengthened by Hannah Arendt's essay "What is Freedom?"—a poignant, sustained lament on the loss of public space within which freedom makes its political appearance in the world. Arendt indicts philosophy's distortion of "the very idea of freedom such as it is given in human experience by transposing it from its original field, the realm of politics and human affairs in general, to an inward domain, the will, where it would be open to self-inspection."[9] Kant is not the initiator but one in a long line of thinkers beginning with Socrates who identified freedom with the free will. This shift from action to willpower, argues Arendt, guaranteed that freedom would remain a "philosophical problem of the first order." But it meant as well that philosophy ongoingly sanctioned loss of space for free action, affirming instead the derivative freedom of willing by a human subject estranged from the world.

No longer a "state of being manifest in action," freedom is relocated within the interstices of the self and the self's inner dialogue.[10] Having abandoned the field of freedom, having retreated from the political realm, the freely willing self "feels" free. For Arendt matters could scarcely be worse for the *raison d'être* "of politics is freedom, and its field of experience is action."[11] Lacking a politically guaranteed public realm, Arendt concludes, freedom cannot make its appearance. She does not find the human heart a secure dwelling place until such time as politics may be possible once again.

If Arendt's discussion is even minimally convincing, Kant's philosophically grand freedom is politically debilitating. Kant's account of moral agency, flowing from his abstract notion of nou-

menal freedom, is similarly baffling if one's eyes are on the look-
out for space for action as a way of being in the world. Kant begins
with a universalism indebted to Christianity's insistence that all
human beings are ensouled and equal in God's eyes. Persons *qua*
human are endowed by Kant with a moral personality defined as
the metaphysical freedom of a rational being who subordinates all
concrete aspects and inclinations to the commands of certain
maxims. In other words, the free, noumenal self is disembodied,
dehistoricized, asocial, stripped of all its ends and objects, shorn
of desires, posited prior to experience, and denuded of all contingencies and particularities. It is this self, this transcendental subject, who freely wills to obey universal moral laws. These stipulations, the Kantian categorical imperatives, cast in universal form,
constitute by definition the rational, moral order.

Kant presumes a transhistorical moral subject. But are all subjects in the same epistemological position? Do all human beings
as noumenal agents apprehend the prescriptive form of the categorical imperatives? Or is it the case that some are more 'noumenal' than others inside the bracing Kantian atmosphere? Recall,
briefly, Kant's insistence that the categorical imperatives are
universal in form and binding in effect upon all without exception.
As rational moral agents, persons *must* act "in conformity with"
the commands of the categorical imperatives. Kantian morality
eliminates by fiat the possibility that a rational moral agent might
face an irreconcilable conflict between competing moral duties and
obligations.

Untethered as noumenal agent to particular ends, objects,
aims, and desires that give rise to conflict, the moral subject obeys
imperatives cast as independent of any social order or historic
forces. Kant offers moral rule-following without conflict, moral
agency without dissent. Moral differences or competing notions of
virtue are not, for Kant, genuine conflicts at all but the result of
confusion and incomplete adherence to the moral law. Bernard
Williams notes, "moral philosophers have discussed what a moral
position is, what a moral argument is, at a very high level of abstraction: being interested in what a moral opinion is *as such*, what
an evaluative opinion is *as such*, they have abstracted on the
whole from the concrete detail of particular sorts of evaluative out-
looks; from the particular sorts of moral concepts that might be
deployed by one group rather than another."[12]

Is the Kantian elimination of moral diversity and conflict, his
promulgation of a rationalized, universalized ethic *particularly*
problematic if the self is female? This seems plausible, first, be-

cause women are less likely to conceive of themselves or to be seen by others as beings free from all considerations of natural and social conditions. Encumbered and defined by the social relations of family life, more tightly linked to embodied experience, culturally constituted in a symbolic and mimetic relation to 'Nature', it was surely difficult to see eighteenth-century women as abstract Kantian subjects nullifying the effects of "special contingencies."[13]

To be sure, the vision of a rational being prior to and independent of his objects and experiences creates difficulties across the board, not to or for women alone. Argues Michael Sandel, this notion of self finally collapses as the Kantian subject is severed from his situation, emerging disembodied, disinterested, and disempowered. But I am most concerned with what Kantian rationalism holds in store for the female self. Caroline Whitbeck, a philosopher, argues that rationalized accounts of moral experience that give no weight to embodiment, or go even further in requiring that the individual sever herself from embodiment, cannot begin to get at complexities of women's embodied experiences. Women have "special bodily experiences" that augment and enhance particular feelings, attitudes, fantasies, and capacities—most importantly those that "induce people generally to care for their infants."[14] The experiences of which Whitbeck writes fall through the grid of rationalist constructions.

Even in the present, women's bodily experiences are "often regarded as unspeakable," whether among philosophers, or between men and women more generally. Women are enjoined either to keep quiet about the topic at the risk of appearing irrational (and morally suspect) or to join the chorus by proclaiming they, too, can abstract themselves from contingent circumstance. Her point is not to insist women are imbedded completely in the embodied and the contingent and can never sort out anything—becoming a being Sandel describes as "in constant danger of drowning in a sea of circumstance."[15] Rather, it is that women tend to see themselves and are seen by others as suspect because they are too clearly embodied and this gets construed as a weakness, not a possible source of moral virtues.

This brings me to a second cluster of reasons women become a suspect category within a Kantian framework. Kant gives the emotions little moral weight, finding human emotions unreliable from the point of view of rational morality. For example, Kant sees sympathy and compassion as untrustworthy and capricious. The emotions lie outside the realm of reason. As the culturally defined more emotional and less rationally rule-governed being, women fall under a cloud. Kant's theory of the emotions or, more properly, his location of the emotions as a brake to moral reasoning, suggests that Kant regarded women as more imbedded in the immediate, hence, less reliably rational.[16]

There is another interesting dimension to this problem: sympathy, compassion, and mercy are downgraded as moral virtues. But other qualities associated historically with women are advanced as "complementary virtues," namely charm, docility, and obedience.[17] To find a woman's virtue in charm is to trivialize the meaning of virtue. Rakes and rapists may be charming. Charm is not so much an achieved attribute of character as the unearned attractiveness of sometimes shallow beings. Even as they charm us, we rightly suspect charming individuals: they are guilty until proven innocent of dishonorable intentions. Kant here downgrades women as moral beings. If woman's charm is celebrated, her obedience is demanded. She must obey not only the moral law but her husband. Docile compliance, however, is not highly visible in lists of the moral virtues.[18]

It is perhaps with this, or something similar in mind (for the ideas noted above were in the air) that Mary Wollstonecraft, in her introduction to A Vindication of the Rights of Woman (published in 1792), celebrated the "manly virtues," those which ennoble "the human character," expressing the hope that women might "every day grow more and more masculine."[19] Women, having been morally trivialized by the flattery of "their *fascinating* graces" and viewed "as if they were in a state of perpetual childhood" are, in fact, unable to stand alone.[20] Wollstonecraft set out to "persuade women to endeavor to acquire strength, both of mind and body, and to convince them that the soft phrases, susceptibility of heart, delicacy of sentiment, and refinement of taste, are almost synonymous with epithets of weakness, and that those beings who are only the objects of pity and that kind of love, which has been termed its sister, will soon become objects of contempt."[21] Wollstonecraft's project makes sense in context because moral courage, in the rationalist frame, is a manly virtue. Observing this linkage, Wollstonecraft could only urge women to become as men rather than to deconstruct the deeper edifice on which this account of the virtues was erected.[22]

One additional reason for women's morally dubious character and situation lies in Kant's account of the "law of domestic society" which provides for the wife's legal possession by her husband. This "liberty of possession" extends to the physical or phenomenal being: thus the runaway wife can be compelled to return to her husband (and the child to a parent, the servant to a master).[23] Possession of a corporeal being, in Kant's view, does not rest on mere coercion or power to command but on "proprietary interest" and "right."[24] This proprietary right, for Kant, is fully compatible with each person's noumenal freedom and equality, for these define the person as such. If one descends from this rarified perch, however, it seems plausible that possession by another—even if of one's empirically situated or embodied self only—downgrades one's moral status in fact whatever Kant argues in theory.

Rationalism and 'the Woman Question'

The refrain—men the reasonable, women the emotional—is familiar and tedious. We are probably also bored by now with feminist arguments that disclaim all tautly drawn gender linkages. But perhaps another look at the matter is worthwhile because of the often problematic ways in which feminist thinkers, determined to prove that women *can* think, sometimes wind up affirming the *understanding* of reason espoused within rationalist theorizing, whether Kant's or that of the explicitly feminist John Stuart Mill.

Mill's nineteenth-century liberal rationalism, different in many important ways from Kantian formulations, nonetheless winds up opposing reason and passion. That which is not Reason is Instinct, Mill writes, and "the worse rather than the better part of human nature."[25] Mill assumes a unity of moral beliefs among individuals dominated by reason. His goal is to couch the principles of moral and political "science" in the form of natural science, a kind of streamlined language of rationalism. For ultimately, according to Mill, "reason speaks in one voice." That voice, historically, was male. In practice, Mill's injunction means that the ignorant or the irrational, those yet to be brought under the rule of reason, will, once having been absorbed, speak in the established, hegemonic rational voice.[26] For Mill there are but two options: the "apotheosis of Reason" or the "idolatry of Instinct." If one begins from this vantage point, the realm of 'necessity' or 'nature' to which women historically were tied is devalued in favor of some sphere of pure (or nearly so) freedom.

As I noted above, one response to all this is to draw women into the world of Reason and Freedom as erected on the basis of a contrast between Instinct (passion, emotion) and Unfreedom (nature, instinct). But this perpetuates the soil in which sexism has been rooted. Carol McMillan argues that "it is a rationalist prejudice that masculine activities depend on agency in a way that traditional, domestic feminine activities do not."[27] To respond to rationalist prejudice against women by insisting women, too, can be 'rational' is just one, and not the most challenging, way to respond to reason's reign.

Alternatively, contextual visions of morality that acknowledge moral diversity and conflict and resist the reduction of ethical life to a set of formal propositions have been proffered by several contemporary feminist thinkers.[28] Their work counters the dichotomy that makes "women. . .the bearers of ignorance and men of knowledge."[29] Dismantling the Enlightenment vision (Kant being one of its leading lights) in which women are "conceptualized as dangerous because less amenable to the guiding light of reason," moral contextualists try to juggle strong ethical principles with real human contingencies.[30]

Contextual moralities are more Aristotelian than Kantian, a difference of form and substance. A contextualized morality does not, as do the rationalists, oversimplify human moral claims and conflicts. One attempt to sketch the markers of a contextualized morality with recent feminist debates in mind begins with the presumption that one cannot discuss moral principles outside of a concrete situation; that morality is best understood as a set of judgments we pass on action rather than abstract, formal rules; that morality is part of a human being's character and virtue a disposition; that concern with purity of moral motivation is inadequate and relatively unimportant in many cases.[31] Those feminist moralists challenging the terms of received rationalisms—in the name of an embodied reason unsevered from life as lived—present a more reflective set of possibilities, political and philosophic, than those proffered by feminists who embrace rationalism's legacy wholesale.

Although women have been the most visible suspect category within the rationalist worldview, they were rarely excluded definitionally or shoved out of the moral landscape altogether. Others, however, were and many of them, or their spokespersons, are now challenging and questioning the use of reason or rationality as a weapon by the dominant or the prejudiced to exclude, to subjugate, and to marginalize. Those once labeled idiots, imbeciles, and morons, for example, are struggling for recognition as moral beings.

Thus we read in the the monthly bulletin issued by the Bureau for Exceptional Children and Adults of the Catholic Archdiocese of Springfield, Massachusetts, that the new Code of Canon Law speaks of "the use of reason" defined "operationally" as the ability to "distinguish the body of Christ from ordinary food" in order that one might participate in the sacrifice of the Eucharist. The Sisters of Jericho House, the name for the bureau's headquarters, find their emotions roused by the phrase "the use of reason," which they describe as "troublesome" and "very hard to tolerate for those of us with mentally retarded friends." Resisting any legal connotation of reason, they proclaim "there are different ways of knowing something or someone," for example, "symbolically or intuitively" or "in communion with the actions of parents." They conclude that no human being is "an isolated unit of intellect and will" and "no one ever believes all alone." It follows that if a retarded child or adult can relate to others, he or she is "educable in the faith" and meets the stipulation of canon law: "the use of reason."

This is a poignant example of contextual reasoning, of the self defined *inside* rather than apart from a social network, ushering into a plea for acceptance and recognition of difference and dignity. Sensitive moral reasoning is all around us in that phenomenal world in which we live and breathe and have our being.[32]

Kant on Citizens, Active and Passive

One final Kantian theme, the notion of citizenship, is central to political thought. The citizen is a human being in his or her political aspect. One insistent grievance in the history of feminist discourse is the denial of citizenship to women historically on a number of grounds.[33] By exploring Kant's views on citizenship, my interpretation comes full circle in this sense: not only are women excluded but the terms under which men are citizens are problematic.

For Kant the citizen is characterized by civic equality and independence which means he owes his "existence and support, not to the arbitrary will of another person...but rather to his own rights and powers...."[34] The fact that one is *qua* person autonomous, rational, free, and self-willing within Kant's metaphysic does not suffice to qualify one for citizenship within his political philosophy. For the acquisition of a "civic personality" a further criterion is needed, namely, that one be an "active part" of the commonwealth, that one be one's own master, and that one "own some sort of property."[35] Specific categories of persons excluded from citizenship on the grounds that they are "mere operatives" include domestic servants, shop clerks, laborers, and "even hairdressers."[36] The disqualification of such persons stems from their placement within the system of social stratification. But there are two additional major categories of persons who are dependent for their support on others: "all women" and children. Kant terms their disqualification a "natural" one. Thus Kant fuses the condition of a priori moral autonomy and freedom with an objective condition of dependence and a "natural" disqualification for public life.

To take some of the edge off his exclusion of categories of persons from an active role in the commonwealth, either on the basis of a natural condition become social fact and legal right (women) or on the basis of occupational status (servants, etc.), Kant divides the category citizen into *active* and *passive*. This strains matters unconvincingly. By denying to women and other "dependent" persons a civil personality—they are "all mere underlings of the commonwealth"—Kant denies them citizenship. Although, as the passive part of the state, such beings can demand they be treated in accord with natural freedom, this freedom in practice "is quite consistent with the greatest inequality in the quantity and degree of...possessions...."[37]

There are other problems. Kant's active citizen is enjoined to be an obedient subject. He has the right to vote and to participate in legally sanctioned activities involving civil society, but the space Kant allows for such politics is narrow and formal. Most importantly, the citizen owes unquestioning obedience to the law as a system of duties. The ghost of Luther haunts Kantian politics as Kant continues: the law compels in 'externals'. If a citizen should decide that a particular law is unjust or that a ruler is guilty of high crimes and misdemeanors, he is reduced to a passivity consonant with obedience to the law as a formal principle.

Following Luther, Kant urges the citizen to maintain silence, to endure suffering, and not to presume to punish a corrupt or unjust ruler. There is no right of sedition, much less a right of revolution, and the slightest attempt to take the life of the sovereign is high treason. "It is the people's duty to endure even the most intolerable abuse of supreme authority."[38] In his discussions of the citizen and polity Kant blends, without acknowledging any tension, strictures against servility, attacks on older forms of paternalistic rule because in them citizens are treated as "mere children" with a requirement that citizens obey the law in all cases. Any active resistance against unjust authority and repressive laws requires punishment, destruction, or exile "in accordance with laws of that authority."[39]

Yet Kant also recognizes that there are times when revolutions succeed. Should one occur, and a new constitution be established, "the illegitimacy of its beginning and of its success cannot free subjects from being bound to accept the new order of things as good citizens, and they cannot refuse to honor and obey the suzerain who now possesses the authority."[40] Why? Because the *form* for law has been reestablished and conformity to external rules is demanded. Kant disallows the possibility that citizens might undertake, as a *moral* obligation, resistance to public authority that may adhere to legal formalities yet engage in repression of its people.[41] His blanket insistence that de facto power acquires de jure legitimacy so long as it promulgates law as a formal requisite is incompatible with the notion of a citizen as a participatory member of a political community.

Ernst Troeltsch writes that the Lutheranism of the Enlightenment—and Kant is among that number—produced much that was good, including "inwardness of ethical autonomy, and depth of feeling in philosophical speculation, but it changed nothing in social doctrines. In practice even Kant, with his respect for authority, thought in Lutheran categories. They then became official and secular in character." He goes on to argue that in the nineteenth century, when such notions of passive obedience to authority revived, they "became a weapon in the hands of a ruling class," producing a blend of "masculine hardness and class-conscious ruthlessness...."[42]

Hannah Arendt claims controversially in her *Eichmann in Jerusalem* that Eichmann, being tried for his role in the Nazi "final solution" to the "Jewish question," declared that he had lived his whole life according to Kant's moral precepts. Of course, Arendt argues, it is outrageous to presume Eichmann had any deep knowledge of Kant and his philosophy. But he did have approximately the right notion of the categorical imperative "translated into popular understanding" and distorted to supplant the "moral law" with "the Führer"; thus, "act in such a way that the Führer, if he knew your action, would approve it." Going beyond obedience, this active evocation of a perversion of the categorical imperative required identification of the moral will of each with a principle beyond the law—the triumph of the will in the *Führerprinzip*.[43]

Finally, there is nothing intrinsic to Kant's philosophy that precludes a constitution from becoming a hollow shell within which citizens have forsworn substantive choice and relinquished their power and duty to make judgments of laws and rulers. If reverence for the moral law may be protected and preserved by acquiescence to abuse of power by those who govern the state, we risk saving our rational wills but losing our humanity. Kant nevertheless may be right—that acquiescence *is* the soundest guarantor of support for "the idea of the state." Perhaps that suggests a lesson very different from Kant's: not that we should obey in order to guarantee the state's existence, putting our faith in the certainty of that teleology of progress in which Kant placed his, but that the "idea of the state" itself must be challenged and changed. For the years since Kant have taught us many sobering lessons, not least of which is the lesson that passive obedience to public authority often results in a politics of barbarism or sterility.

Notes

1. Carol Gilligan, *In a Different Voice* (Cambridge, Mass.: Harvard University Press, 1982).
2. Although Immanuel Kant (1724–1800) somewhat antedates Jean-Jacques Rousseau (1712–1778), who is the subject of Chapter 4 below, I am taking up Kant first because of the inner connection between his and Luther's understanding of the self and freedom.
3. Gilligan's analysis has its own problems of dehistoricization and depolitization but she has hit upon a genuine vexation and opened debate in a fruitful way.
4. I will not take up at length the enormously complicated question of the historic role rationalist discourse played in restructuring political life along bureaucratic lines; nor shall I treat, save obliquely, twentieth-century rationalism's dominance of political discourse. My aim is to contemplate the Kantian 'moment' and its shaping of our understandings of the self and the world of the self.
5. Hannah Arendt, *The Life of the Mind* (New York: Harcourt, Brace Jovanovich, 1978), p. 43.
6. Immanuel Kant, *Critique of Pure Reason*, trans. Norman Kemp Smith (New York: The Modern Library, 1958), p. 195. Women are in trouble already given their particular corporeality, a question I turn to below. Portions of this chapter are drawn from my essay, "Kant, Politics, and Persons: The Implications of his Moral Philosophy," *Polity* 14 (Winter 1981):205–21.
7. Kant, *Critique of Pure Reason*, pp. 257, 259.
8. Ibid., p. 257.
9. The essay appears in the collection *Between Past and Future* (Baltimore: Penguin Books, 1968), p. 145.
10. Ibid., passim. Interestingly, Arendt exempts Jesus of Nazareth from her general indictment of Christianity's anti-political tendencies. For Jesus' sayings in the New Testament show "an extraordinary understand-

ing of freedom, and particularly of the power inherent in human freedom,"
p. 168.

11. Ibid., p. 146.

12. "Conversation with Bernard Williams: Philosophy and Morals,"
in *Modern British Philosophy*, ed. Bryan Magee (New York: St. Martin's
Press, 1971), p. 153.

13. Michael J. Sandel, *Liberalism and the Limits of Justice* (Cambridge: Cambridge University Press, 1982), p. 114. Sandel's elegant critique of a Kantian-derived deontological liberalism is must reading for anyone concerned with these questions.

14. Caroline Whitbeck, "The Maternal Instinct," in *Mothering: Essays
in Feminist Theory*, ed. Joyce Trebilcot (Totowa, N.J.: Rowman and Allanheld, 1984), pp. 185–92, 191.

15. Sandel, *Liberalism and Limits of Justice*, p. 57.

16. Lawrence A. Blum, "Kant's and Hegel's Moral Rationalism: A
Feminist Perspective," *Canadian Journal of Philosophy* 12 (June
1982):287–302, 289.

17. Ibid., p. 291.

18. Interestingly, Kant's theory of citizenship for males also pushes
toward passivity in relation to authority, a point I argue below.

19. Mary Wollstonecraft, *A Vindication of the Rights of Woman* (New
York: W. W. Norton, 1967), p. 33.

20. Ibid., p. 34.

21. Ibid.

22. Wollstonecraft is not uncritically supportive of "manly virtue,"
finding nothing attractive in "hunting, shooting, and gaming" to the extent these are considered masculine verities.

23. Immanuel Kant, *Groundwork of the Metaphysic of Morals*, trans.
H. J. Paton (New York: Harper Torchbook, 1969), p. 69. Cf. Mary J. Gregor,
Laws of Freedom (Oxford: Basil Blackwell, 1963), pp. 50–51.

24. For a more complete discussion see Elshtain, "Kant, Politics and
Persons," pp. 211–14.

25. John Stuart Mill, *On the Subjection of Women* (Greenwich,
Conn.: Fawcett, 1973), p. 18. I draw on my discussion of Mill in *Public
Man, Private Woman* for these comments on Mill.

26. See Graeme Duncan, *Marx and Mill: Two Views of Social Conflict and Social Harmony* (Cambridge: Cambridge University Press, 1973),
p. 262.

27. Carol McMillan, *Women, Reason and Nature* (Oxford: Basil Blackwell, 1982), p. 99. McMillan's book has been much maligned as reaction-
ary by some rationalist feminists who do not see the deeper philosophic
issues at stake here.

28. For example: Gilligan's book, *In a Different Voice*, however halt-
ingly, can be seen in this light. As well, Sara Ruddick's essay, "Maternal
Thinking," in *Mothering: Essays in Feminist Theory*, ed. Joyce Trebilcot
(Totowa, N.J.: Rowman and Allenheld, 1984), pp. 213–30 is a good
example.

29. L. J. Jordanova, "Natural Facts: A Historical Perspective on Science and Sexuality," in *Nature, Culture and Gender*, ed. Carol P. Mac-Cormack and Marilyn Strathern (Cambridge: Cambridge University Press 1980), pp. 42–69, 43.

30. The quote is from ibid., p. 67.

31. Joan Tronto, "The Scottish Enlightenment, Contextual Morality, and Current Feminist Debate" (Paper presented at the 1984 meeting of the American Political Science Association). Of course, contextual morality may itself become an abstract relativism, a danger one must think about and guard against.

32. It is sad but true that most of us most of the time are insensitive to terms of social exclusion unless we or someone we love or know is directly affected. My concern with the retarded, or "developmentally different" in current usage, began when my oldest daughter was diagnosed, at the age of three, as "mildly retarded." Over the years, as I read the words of many abstract philosophers, I realized: "They don't think Sheri is human." I knew then, if I hadn't understood before, that there was something terribly wrong with their philosophies.

33. Susan Moller Okin, in *Women in Western Political Thought* (Princeton: Princeton University Press, 1979), discusses some of the grounds for denial of citizenship historically.

34. Immanuel Kant, *The Metaphysical Elements of Justice* (Indianapolis: Bobbs-Merrill, 1965), p. 78.

35. Ibid.

36. Immanuel Kant, *On the Old Saw: That May be Right in Theory But It Won't Work in Practice* (Philadelphia: University of Pennsylvania Press, 1974), p. 63.

37. Ibid., p. 60.

38. Kant, *Metaphysical Elements Justice*, p. 86.

39. Ibid., p. 84

40. Ibid., p. 89.

41. Kant, *Old Saw*, p. 67.

42. Ernst Troeltsch, *The Social Teachings of the Christian Churches*, vol. 2 (Chicago: University of Chicago Press, 1981), p. 544.

43. Hannah Arendt, *Eichmann in Jerusalem* (New York: Penguin Books, 1963), pp. 135–37.

4

Rousseau Redux:
Bodies Social and Political

One does not begin by reasoning, but by feeling.
Jean-Jacques Rousseau

Rousseau haunts contemporary political thinking. If not all things to all people, he is many things to many people. There are as many Rousseaus as there are Rousseau readers and controversies continue to swirl around his head. From Mary Wollstonecraft's rejoinders in 1792, to contemporary attacks on Rousseau as a misogynist, his work has provoked feminist thinkers. That forms one section in an enormous, many-colored Rousseauian patchwork quilt. To Rousseau's sexual politics one must add his sophisticated speculations on the origin of language, his theories of sexual and psychological development, his confessionals, his novels of romantic sensibility, his anthropology and political economy, his advice to constitution-drafters, and his most famous treatise on politics, *The Social Contract*.[1] In an earlier work, I concentrated on Rousseau's arguments concerning the relationship between "virtuous families and just polities," and I noted, as well, the importance Rousseau assigns to emotions and to the imagination.[2]

Fortunately, Rousseau is so rich and various a thinker one can rethink his work without fear of repeating oneself. Each re-reading yields fresh insights. Whatever the conceptual yield of these return engagements, Rousseau's greatness as a prose stylist, his volubility and daring, invigorate the reader, students and teachers alike. A consistent pattern has emerged in my courses in "Modern Political Thought": the time allotted on the syllabus to Rousseau always expands. Students are more intrigued by Rousseau than anyone else (Freud is a close contender) and have more to say as a consequence.

My emphases in the discussion below reflect closely the kinds of issues I have raised with my students, and they with me, over the past several years of 'thinking Rousseau'. If there is a general theme that unites the separate portions of the interpretation to follow it is that of the embodied self: natural, social, political. For Rousseau is a great materialist. He never forgets that we are embodied beings and that our bodies are the ground of our identities, signaling who we are, what our limits and possibilities might be, what diciplines and indulgences do to or for our bodies, how civilization inscribes itself on the human body, and so on. Controversially, he insists that the markers and meaning of embodied identity *must* vary for males and females in ways reflected in, and shaped by, social forms.

In the Beginning . . . the Body

The most hotly contested feature of Rousseau's theory of embodiment in recent years is the matter of sex differences and the difference they do (or do not) make. But there are other themes of embodiment in Rousseau that may in the long run be more important to our understanding of civilization's mixed blessings than what he has to say about male and female bodies. I have in mind his history of human embodiment, a complex, ethical account of human bodies in nature, through the earliest rudimentary forms of social life, and into civilization proper.

But, first, what about male and female? Rousseau's is a complex view. He does *not* endorse a reductive biological determinism. On this score Rousseau is quite explicit, noting (in *The Second Discourse),* that human beings alone among animals can "choose" or "reject" the surgings of impulse through acts of freedom. What really distinguishes us from our fellow creatures, he argues, is not our lofty capacity to reason—Rousseau being one of the great deflaters of Enlightenment rationalism—nor even our greater sense and understanding since other animals have sense and understanding too, but our consciousness of our freedom to go along with or to resist the impetus of instinct. "Nature commands every animal," he writes, "and the beast obeys. Man feels the same impetus, but he realizes that he is free to acquiesce or resist. . . .[3] We feel the same thing as the "beast" but we have a "power of willing" unknown to those with whom we co-habit the earth.[4] Rousseau credits human beings, male and female, with a "very specific quality," "the faculty of self-perception."

Neither males nor females, then, are simple creatures of instinct but they are distinct from one another, a distinction that occurs in nature and sets the basis for later socially constituted distinctions including, finally, the different parts men and women play in the human drama in all its complexity. Culturally demarcated distinctions between the sexes, social and natural, are not for Rousseau "the result of mere prejudice, but of reason."[5] The education Rousseau provides for his Emile and Sophie, respectively, for "man" and "woman" in an archetypal sense, involves strong markers of sex differences, not crudely to keep women "in their place" but in order to sustain a vision of sexual interdependence based upon sexual differentiation. Women are by no means powerless in this scheme of things but their forms of power and those of men differ in scope and form. The man alone bears legitimate or formal authority; the woman exercises power in a variety of individual and culturally ritualized, yet informal ways. (For example: women sustain communal life through gossip which serves to bind communities together, to censure 'deviants', to sustain order.)

Part of what is going on when Rousseau builds on sex differences is a link between male physical strength and military service. I will turn to this dimension of his thinking below. But he also wants to construct a scheme of things in which both men and women choose, and are content with, sexually active but "chaste" unions. He perceives harmful individual and social consequences from promiscuity, particularly for women. Sexual equilibrium, including a shared commitment to monogamy, is made possible only when women stress their differences from men: in this way they gain power over men and exert their influence. Women have the means to neutralize disparities in physical strength and size and they should take advantage of these means, Rousseau insists, for they are the more vulnerable sex, most notably when they are pregnant and later nursing a fragile infant.[6]

Within Rousseau's discourse, women are great initiators of civilized, settled life.[7] Rousseau's men and women need love; they need one another. Family ties that emerge flow from revolutionary "developments of the heart" and give rise to the "sweetest sentiments known to men," "conjugal and paternal" [sic] love, embody (quite literally) fructifying possibilities. Minimally, the intimate family serves as a corrective to destructive, privatizing individualism.[8] Yet the historic creation of the moralized family also makes

men dependent upon women in ways that enhance male vulnerability and *may*, if the society is decadently overcivilized, threaten
the loss of those civic virtues Rousseau cherishes most—of which
more below.

I noted in the preceding chapter that women are a suspect category from the standpoint of a strong, incorporeal rationalism.
Women are not thus "suspect" in Rousseau's embodied
account—not a priori—but they are "different." They become suspect, in one part of Rousseau's teaching, because they draw men
into interdependencies which, though essential to civilization, also
make men frighteningly vulnerable. As well, those women cor-
rupted by decadent 'society' act as agents of corruption more
generally—thus Rousseau's often tedious polemicizing against the
ladies of Paris. Interestingly, each of these commentaries involves
recognition of female social power though it casts that power nega-
tively and, to our eyes, unfairly, Sexuality, for Rousseau, is a potent and "terrible" passion; it must be restrained. In a true love
relationship, physical and moral elements comingle. Women are
vital agents of this process, for they establish their ascendancy
when love fixes on a single object—when intimacy is moralized.
Promiscuity, particularly in adolescent males, must be sublimated
into a moral relationship. Moralized sexuality became a possibility for humans given our species evolutionary shift from the estrus
cycle to ongoing sexual receptivity.

The sexual-socialized interdependence of males and females
stressed by Rousseau (and, remember, he both extols it and laments it) is the subject of much of Mary Wollstonecraft's critique.
For, argues Wollstonecraft, Rousseau's insistence that women
must accentuate difference in order to have power over men is destructive to men and women alike. The more women demand to
be educated like men, claims Rousseau, and the more women become like men, the less influence they will have over men and at
that point "men will be masters indeed," untouched by the more
compassionate sex.[9] Rousseau's belief that equality must be based
on difference, requiring therefore interdependence between the
sexes, is for Wollstonecraft a delusion. For Wollstonecraft differences must be diminished if not altogether negated in order that
men and women stand face-to-face as "rational creatures" acquir-
ing the same "human virutes" by the same means. Otherwise,
women will be "educated like a fanciful kind of *half* being—one of
Rousseau's wild chimeras."[10]

For Wollstonecraft "the sexual distinction which men have so
warmly insisted upon is arbitrary," and lies at the root of "female

follies."[11] Whatever the strengths of Wollstonecraft's indictment
of society's manners and mores and the ways in which they exag-
gerate a version of the sexual distinction that constitutes women
as less honorable beings than men—and they are many—she does
not wrestle with the question of difference, of embodiment itself,
in the depth of Rousseau's discourse.

To repeat: Rousseau never lets us forget that personal identity
is in some fundamental sense bodily identity—that we are never
not our bodies and whether our bodies are male or female is important, not trivial, in the forging of identity. The contemporary vision of equality between the sexes Rousseau can be drawn upon
to support is one that acknowledges differences yet insists upon
full legal and civil equality. In the next section I will once again pit
Wollstonecraft against Rousseau in a discussion of sensibility and
the imagination.

I described Rousseau as an "ethical anthropologist." He tells
a story of human beings as evolving animals with the body's needs
and imperatives transforming over time. Rousseau offers intimations of a "history of the body." He argues, for example, that our
eating habits have changed—and not for the better—for humans
are naturally frugivorous, not carnivorous.[12] In his notes to the
Second Discourse, he observes that "anatomical observations confirm" the view that human beings have "teeth and intestines like
those of frugivorous animals...."[13] These early observations receive ongoing confirmation from contemporary paleo-
anthropologists. As further proof of our frugivorous inclinations,
Rousseau observes in *Emile* the indifference of children to meat,
and their preference for dairy products and vegetables; clearly,
"the taste for meat is not natural to man...."[14] Rousseau argues
that children should not be forced to become carnivores. "If this
is not for their health, it is for their character; for, however one explains the experience, it is certain that great eaters of meat are in
general more cruel and ferocious than other men."[15]

At first glance Rousseau's indictment of meat-eating may seem
simply eccentric—the ravings of a "veggie" zealot. But take another look. There is a warning in all this talk of frugivorous and
carnivorous diets. The warning is that when we push the body
against a powerful disposition there will always be costs, individual
and social. These costs will be inscribed in and on the body itself
and marked, as well, in social deformations.

As this story has been played out in our own time, we see the
costs dramatically. Our heavily meat-oriented diet is implicated in
a plethora of human illnesses, particularly cancer and heart dis-

ease. Human ailments, Rousseau insisted, are no simple tale of microbes but a complex social story. We know, he observed, that many diseases are the direct product of civilization. He writes: "With regard to illnesses, I shall not repeat the vain and false declamations against medicine made by most people in good health; rather, I shall ask whether there is any solid observation from which one might conclude that in countries where this art is most neglected, the average life of man is shorter than in those where it is cultivated with greatest care. And how could that be, if we give ourselves more ills than medicine can furnish remedies?"[16]

One further implication of Rousseau's insistence that we are meant to be grain and vegetable eaters is the fact that this story undercuts the terrifying foundational myth of man the hunter that has so dominated our imaginations. Portraying our ancestor as a vicious naked ape, a killer of animals and eater of meat, we are told that the males protected and provided for the women and the kids through their hunting and ferocity. But Rousseau's narrative of origins invites us to think of collectivities of males, females, and infants engaged primarily in foraging and plant raising. Women are central actors in this human story, not frightened dependents huddled in the cave waiting for the animal carcass to be brought through the entrance-way by the he-hunters.

One face of Jean-Jacques, then, is that of the critical social ecologist. He warns that advance in our knowledge promises—and threatens—to bring us so much power that we may, in the end, ruin everything by trying to become sole masters of the universe.[17] This is central to his indictment of civilization, a ruination brought about by attempts to gain absolute control. Rousseau seeks no simple return "to nature"—we can never go back in that sense, he knows, and he anticipates the *reductio ad absurdum* to which his critics will take his arguments by crying: "What! must we destroy societies, annihilate thine and mine, and go back to live in forests with bears? A conclusion in the manner of my adversaries, which I prefer to anticipate rather than leave them the shame of drawing it."[18] This objection is absurd—as Rousseau's poking fun at it shows. We cannot go back. But, knowing how we have been shaped, knowing our passions are no longer simple, knowing we can no longer nourish ourselves on grass and nuts, nor do without political authority, we can, at least, respect the "sacred bonds" of the societies of which we are members; we can love and serve our fellow human beings; and we can resist a phony innocence about power and control and its supposed unlimited capacity for good we most often call progress. Over two hundred years before we officially entered an "environmental crisis," Rousseau understood that "unhealthy trades...shorten lives or destroy the physique, such as labor in mines, various preparations of metals and minerals,...others working in quarries" and so on.[19]

Here Rousseau joins contemporary critics of culture. For example, Wendell Berry, the poet and essayist, claims, in a Rousseauian vein, that the "isolation of the body" is "the fundamental damage of the specialist system." We put bodies to tasks that insult the mind and demean the spirit. We give the body over to specialists if something goes wrong even as we "find it easier than ever to prefer our own bodies to the bodies of other creatures and to abuse, exploit and otherwise hold in contempt those other bodies for the greater good or comfort of our own."[20] Michel Foucault argues that the body is the inscribed surface of events—that the nervous system, digestive apparatus, and so on, are scarred by modern life. If it is the task of genealogy, in Foucault's sense, "to expose a body totally imprinted by history and the process of history's destruction of the body," Rousseau is a master genealogist who offers a history of the present (his own epoch), warning and enlightening us about the embodied deformations of our world. It is this Rousseau who shall have the final word:

> If you consider the mental anguish that consumes us, the violent passions that exhaust and desolate us, the excessive labors with which the poor are overburdened, the still more dangerous softness to which the rich abandon themselves, and which cause the former to die of their needs and the latter of their excesses; if you think of the monstrous mixtures of foods, their pernicious seasonings, corrupted foodstuffs, falsified drugs, the knavery of those who sell them, the errors of those who administer them, the poison of the containers in which they are prepared; if you pay attention to the epidemic illnesses engendered by the bad air among the multitudes of men gathered together, to the illnesses occasioned by the delicacy of our way of life, by the alternating movements from the interior of our houses into the fresh air, the use of garments put on or taken off with too little precaution, and all the causes that our excessive sensuality has turned into necessary habits, the neglect or privation of which then costs us our life or our health; if you take into account fires and earthquakes which, burning or upsetting whole cities, cause their inhabitants to die by the thousands; in a word, if you unite the dangers that all these causes continually gather over our heads, you will sense how dearly nature makes us pay for the scorn we have shown for its lessons.[21]

Sensibility as Feminized Discourse

In contemporary American society we think of 'manners' as the proper way to handle a salad fork or to pick up a napkin. But there is a much richer notion of manners as social expressions of a way of life. If Jane Austen is a novelist of manners, Rousseau is a theorist of manners. Despite his widely noted expressions of ambivalence toward women, and his indictment of female decadence as signifying the despoilation of civilization, Rousseau is one of the architects and molders of an explicitly feminized sensibility. It makes sense: if women are potent enough to spoil civilization, they are powerful enough to provide coherence and inspiration for a social order as well. If men are incomplete without women the same holds for social life.

The political features of this view will be taken up in the next section. My focus for now is on a subtler though no less interesting set of considerations—Rousseau's creation of a romantic and feminized sensibility. Much of Wollstonecraft's objections to Rousseau are directed at this formation of sentiment.

I begin with Rousseau's stress on feeling—for that is where he begins. Rousseau features no dualist split of mind/body, no noumenal/phenomenal divide of the sort central to Kant's moral theory. For Rousseau, our corporealism and our moral being are intimates, just as philosophic thought may originate in feelings and dreams rather than abstract stipulations. As James Miller argues in his recent work, Rousseau was a man who had a unique ability to express his dreams, to make them memorable, to justify them and to communicate them to a broad audience hoping thereby to enlist others in new hopes, desires, and intimations.[22] Rousseau celebrates and gives vivid life to the workings of the imagination. He is a fantasist, drawing upon a repertoire of complexly intermingled private and public imaginings in his own work.[23] He describes states of agitation "bordering on delirium" as the matrix of his political writing.[24] Rousseau's self-characterized transports strike the modern eye as excessive and 'feminine'. That is, we have inherited an image of women, far more than men, as beings given over to, or giving themselves over to, excessive sway by emotion and inchoate longings. Rousseau is one of the great architects of this sensibility: he is one of the reasons we associate 'the feminine' with tremulous desirings.

One root to Rousseau's contribution to what became the reigning discourse of sensibility is his theory of language. He begins with powerful feelings of love and pity. Figurative language was the first to be born and the initial stirrings of language speak to and from our human desire for recognition and love—words grow from moral needs and passions. "At first only poetry was spoken; there was no hint of reasoning until much later," he writes.[25] The distance between Rousseau's understandings and those of the rationalists on the one hand, and nominalists on the other, is great. For Thomas Hobbes, that greatest of nominalists, the imagination is nothing but "decaying sense" and words are crudely designative. For John Locke, fantasies mislead the judgment. But Rousseau embraces poetry and fantasy. His own mind, he tells us, was dominated by the pictures it produced.[26]

My recasting of Rousseau's story of human and linguistic origins goes like this: without imagination, without our primordial social inclination of pity or compassion, life would be wholly brutal. For in imagining we take ourselves out of ourselves. We identify with others who suffer. When we feel pity, we depict for ourselves the reality of someone else's pain and if we could not do this, we would not be human. Moments of sharp pity for the sufferings of others; moments of ecstatic reverie—these are sources of enthusiasm for truth and the wellsprings of sensibility. For most of us most of the time scientific discourse is irrelevant. We have more important resources at our command because we can both act and imagine. To presume one can understand reason in too stark and naked a form is an error of Enlightenment arrogance, Rousseau insists, for by impoverishing the imagination one loses the most energetic of all languages and human capacities.[27] Cold rationalism fails to touch the human heart.

Human passions are not simply given. They do not exist as such. Just as human embodiment has a history, so does human feeling. Passions can be educated and context is vital. The milieu in which we find ourselves will determine the education of our sensibility. Structures of mind and feeling change as civilization changes. For example: Rousseau portrays the earliest natural being as one of great feeling and gifted with pity. But this being is also incomplete with reference to a range of human possibilities.[28] With civilization a greater expansiveness of possibility, as well as greater dangers of deformation and a destructive de-naturalization, occur. We must, therefore, struggle to keep sentiment alive and to stoke incessantly the fires of human pity.

To keep sentiment alive—one of the tasks Rousseau assigned to himself—and he was a great master at evoking voluble human emotion in a growing class of bourgeois readers, male and female. This puts a very different spin on one's reading of, say, Sophie's education in Rousseau's *Emile*. To a sensibility informed by liberal political thought and feminist concerns, and shaped by modernity, Sophie's is an education to second-class citizenship and domestic confinement. We read Rousseau's *La Nouvelle Heloise*, and we see a woman—his heroine—doomed unfairly, to our eyes.[29] But the way Rousseau's feminine creations and their sensibility played themselves out historically, and the way Rousseau was read by his own readers, is not captured by these interpretations.

John McManners, for example, demonstrates the ways in which Rousseau's sympathetic insight and "moral fervour, and his Julie captured the imagination of the age as the ideal of womanhood. . . . " Although some feminist writers at the time condemned Rousseau's restrictive notions of womanhood, the vast majority of the many women who read Rousseau, continues McManners, saw a world "dominated by a woman." Julie's "femininity is not an inferior mode of being: it is perfection of its kind."[30] As well, the deeper lesson of the novel is a celebration of freely chosen unions between male and female. Coming at a time when both the Church and writers of the Enlightenment joined to protest arranged marriage, Rousseau confirms that "free choice is the only moral way in personal relationships."[31] In another curious twist, the illiberalism we see in Sophie's education was less important, in the eighteenth century, than the impetus *Emile* and writings of other pedagogical theorists gave to female education. In Rousseau's explicitly political writings. education of girls is necessary to the creation and maintenance of republican civic virtue, a theme I address below.

Women readers in the period from the eighteenth century on mostly read novels, just as the class of women writers mostly wrote novels. The novel is the great creation of a specifically bourgeois identity and sensibility and it presumes, among others, an intimate relation between author and reader. Rousseau is directly implicated in this specifically feminized discourse. In all his works, but most particularly the novels, Rousseau drew his reader into an intimate relation with himself, with "Jean-Jacques." They addressed him directly, penning effusive letters and testimonials to him on a first name basis. Robert Darnton, a cultural historian, argues that the manner in which Rousseau revolutionized the "relation between reader and text" opened "the way to romanticism."[32] Rousseau, Darnton claims, penetrated "into the everyday world" of bourgeois individuals, helping people to make sense of things, particularly matters intimate and familial. His readers credit Rousseau with newly found sweet sentiments, one father writing that he owes his own "tender obligation" as an involved father to "Virtuous Jean-

Jacques!''[33] Rousseau's *Nouvelle Heloise* was "the biggest best-seller of the century. The demand for copies outran the supply so badly that booksellers rented it out by the day and even by the hour. . . ."[34] This break with a prior and more staid sensibility set the basis for political and poetic romanticism—and for the female-dominated novel.

There were dissenters from this sensibility. Re-enter Mary Wollstonecraft who, in addition to being one of the staunchest of Rousseau's feminist critics is also one of his great admirers. Woll-stonecraft concurs with much of Rousseau's condemnation of fe-male pettiness and corrupting influence and she also endorses his insistence that eighteenth-century women, particularly those of the aristocracy and their *bourgeois* imitators, had denatured women in destructive ways, tearing them away from the wellsprings of a more virtuous orientation. With Rousseau, Wollstonecraft advo-cates breast-feeding and a robust maternalism. But she parts com-pany with Rousseau in the manner in which a such a return to fe-male maternal empowerment and virtue is to be achieved. "The mother, who wishes to give true dignity of character to her daugh-ter," writes Wollstonecraft, "must, regardless of the sneers of ig-norance, proceed on a plan diametrically opposite to that which Rousseau has recommended with all the deluding charms of elo-quence and philosophical sophistry; for his eloquence renders ab-surdities plausible, and his dogmatic conclusions puzzle, without convincing, those who have not ability to refute them."[35]

Specifically, Rousseau's pedagogical theory undercuts his im-age of female contributions to civic virtue. In educating the girl to be a coquette by overheating what is presumed to be naturally there, by exaggerating a sex difference that stresses female appear-ance and a kind of narcissistic exhibitionism, Rousseau guarantees that women will sink below "the level of rational creatures." "Taught from their infancy that beauty is woman's sceptre, the mind shapes itself to the body, and, roaming round its gilt cage, only seeks to adore its prison."[36] Educated in an "enervating style," women cannot play a vital civic role. Rousseau's romantic sensibility, all tears and swoonings, is but *one* aspect of male iden-tity. But, Wollstonecraft insists, Rousseau guarantees that this sen-sibility will define the whole of the female, thereby perpetuating the very female weaknesses Rousseau himself aptly identifies.

Wollstonecraft's rationalist, liberal feminism undercuts Rous-seau's romanticized and feminized discourse of sensibility. She lo-cates this sensibility as the source of Rousseau's own well-documented miseries: "Why was Rousseau's life divided between ecstasy and misery? Can any other answer be given than this, that the effervescence of his imagination produced both; but, had his fancy been allowed to cool, it is possible that he might have acquired more strength of mind."[37] Wollstonecraft would deconstruct the romantic Jean-Jacques in favor of Citizen Rousseau, the ardent champion of republican virtue, the source of Robespierre's adamantine civic urges. (Though here, too, she had qualms about Rousseau's genealogical construction of that virtue.)

Love of Fatherland and Mother's Milk

Rousseau, as political architect and advocate, has been praised as the father of civic republicanism, a "dreamer of democracy" in Miller's phrase, and condemned as a maven of the monolithic, closed collectivity. As with every other feature of Rousseau's discourse, one can find textual support for both conclusions. I am not so much interested in mediating between these opposed propositions as in looking at specific features of Rousseau's political vision that implicate and require women yet locate women outside the sphere of civic virtue proper. If Jean-Jacques, the romantic, creates a feminized sensibility, Rousseau, the father of the "social contract" and the consultant to writers of constitutions, defeminizes politics. All this needs explaining.

Perhaps the best place to begin is with a reminder. For Rousseau, to be a citizen is to undergo a dramatic civic transformation. His is a robust understanding of what citizenship is and requires. The man-become-citizen gives himself to the polity and internalizes an absolutely binding civic religion with demanding articles of faith.[38] The citizen must prefer the life of the body politic to that of his own body and when the state demands it he must forfeit his life. The "moral and collective body," "this public person" takes precedence.[39]

Virtuous polities require virtuous families. Children must imbibe love for the fatherland (the *patrie*), with their mother's milk.[40] Romantic love between men and women sets the basis for what might be called the civic family, the family that inculcates a passion for political virtue (although it also, paradoxically, may threaten that virtue if it is too insular and absorbing).[41] Even as the coming together of male and female results in a mutually interdependent particularity, so Rousseau's vision of a body politic, captured in the metaphor of the "general will," constitutes a potent moment of universality. Rousseau sees the nation (in Hannah

Arendt's words) "as a body driven by one will," requiring the overcoming of different and separate wills: from many bodies to *the* Body Politic.[42]

Mother and mother's milk enters at the foundation for a basis that must be provided for civic spiritedness. Thus Rousseau in *Emile*:

> The first education is the most important, and this first education belongs incontestably to women; if the Author of nature had wanted it to belong to men, He would have given them milk with which to nurse the children. . . . The laws—always so occupied with property and so little with persons, because their object is peace not virtue—do not give enough authority to mothers. However, their status is more certain than that of fathers; their duties are more painful; their cares are more important for the good order of the family; generally they are more attached to the children. There are occasions on which a son who lacks respect for his father can in some way be excused. But if on any occasion whatsoever a child were unnatural enough to lack respect for his mother—for her who carried him in her womb, who nursed him with her milk, who for years forgot herself in favor of caring for him alone—one should hasten to strangle this wretch as a monster unworthy of seeing the light of day.[43]

Similarly, Rousseau finds the citizen in whom love of the fatherland as a civic *mother* does not beat steadily and true, a monster, an unworthy wretch. Just as treason to the mother warrants strangulation, treason to the state calls for Draconian punishment, public shaming, and execution. Just as the mother's watchful eyes must be ever on her developing child, so the "citizen shall feel the eyes of his fellow-countrymen upon him every moment of the day; that no man shall move upward and win success except by public approbation; that every post and employment shall be filled in accordance with the nation's wishes; and that everyone—from the least of the nobles, or even the least of the peasants, up to the king himself, if that were possible—shall be so completely dependent upon public esteem as to be unable to do anything, acquire anything, or achieve anything without it."[44]

Mothers figure centrally—but not *as* citizens; rather as the mothers of citizens to-be (males) and mothers to-be of citizens (females). Wollstonecraft cavils at this, insisting that women must be active citizens if they are to pass civic virtue onto their young. Why, then, does Rousseau preclude direct female political participation? The answer lies in the tradition of civic republicanism in

general and in the *terms* of that republicanism in particular in
Rousseau's thought. For Rousseau offers a tautly drawn nexus between being a citizen and bearing arms, a sex-linked civic
difference.

Men alone, as I noted briefly above, have the bodies of
defenders—they alone can serve as soldiers. Women, absorbed
with caring for their own vulnerable infants, cannot go forth to defend the polity through force of arms. He describes the female citizen, in a terrifying passage from *Emile*, Book I, as follows: "A
Spartan woman had five sons in the army and was awaiting news
of the battle. A Helot arrives: trembling, she asks him for news.
'Your five sons were killed.' 'Base slave, did I ask you that?' 'We
won the victory.' The mother runs to the temple and gives thanks
to the gods. This is the female citizen."[45] And in *The Second Discourse*. addressing his own "amiable and virtuous country-
women," Rousseau proclaims it the "fate of your sex . . . to govern
ours. It is fortunate when your chaste power, exercised solely in
conjugal union, makes itself felt only for the glory of the State and
the public happiness! Thus did women command at Sparta and
thus do you deserve to command at Geneva."[46] Patriotism is tied
to conjugal, specifically maternal, imperatives and affections. This
potent love of mother country, and willingness to serve and protect her, will shrivel on the civic vine if mothers no longer figure
so overpoweringly in the affections and upbringings of their
children.

It is important to remind oneself of the context here. Rousseau
is a defender of freedom and the autonomy of bodies-politic. He
fears whatever works to dilute the patriotic tie. The widespread use
of mercenaries, of soldiers paid to fight, is one indication for Rousseau, following Machiavelli, of a loss of civic virtue and a sure sign
the republic is on the wane or already lost. For republican virtue and
freedom to flourish citizen soldiers are required. To this end, women
play a central role but must also be kept in their (honored) place. If
women stray from the pathway of *their* virtue, civic disaster is a
likely result for the loss of republican womanhood is brought about
by a corrupt feminizing.

Rousseau condemns the effeminate and warns men against
"womanish adornment."[47] The glorious republicanism of the an-
cient world was lost in part because of a loss of masculine vigor,
an effeminizing of social life, and the acceptance of a specifically
effeminate and devirilizing religion, Christianity. (Women played
a key part in that, too.) Thus the "Romans admitted that military
virtue died out among them to the degree that they became con-

noisseurs of paintings, engravings, jeweled vessels, and began to cultivate the fine arts."[48] Rousseau's free republic requires citizen armies.

Wollstonecraft will have none of this; better, she wants the virtue without the martial dimensions.[49] If a nation were forced into a truly just war, she argues, women too would be patriotically aroused and do their part. She shared a vision of civic motherhood. But Rousseau, in her view, celebrates not virtue but "barbarism." He valorizes the Romans who conquered and destroyed but did not extend "the reign of virtue." He "exalts those to demi-gods who were scarcely human—the brutal Spartans, who, in defiance of justice and gratitude, sacrificed, in cold blood, the slaves who had shewn themselves heroes to rescue their oppressors."[50]

In his rush to rescue virtue from vice, Rousseau misidentified virtue. He missed the truly "gigantic mischief" of arbitrary power and "hereditary distinctions" that, together with "a standing army" are "incompatible with freedom." At this point, Wollstonecraft seems our contemporary in her warning that "subordination" is a chief sinew of "military discipline" and that "despotism is necessary to give vigour" to the military enterprise. Romantic notions of honor may be apt for the commanding few but the vast majority of soldiers are a mass swept along by coercion and command. How can this possibly serve as a model of virtue? Whatever one thinks of Wollstonecraft's characterization of armies, her astute recognition that the entire tradition of civic republicanism from Machiavelli through Rousseau assimilates civic and martial virtues and, in so doing, guarantees the civic incapacity of women remains salient today as we think about what political equality between the sexes implies or requires by way of responsibilities as well as rights and privileges.

Even if one follows Wollstonecraft in rejecting Rousseau's martial vision of civic virtue, it is impossible, unless one indulges in massive wishful thinking, to evade Rousseau's troubling and stubborn insistence that we cannot have it both ways: we cannot celebrate a robust individualism for *all*, on the one hand, and extol the virtues of community, on the other. By placing before us at every point the fact that constraints are necessary if people are to live together, rather than live as isolates *among* one another, Rousseau nags at us. We sense that if despotism takes root it does so more readily if a people is already fragmented and primarily self-seeking. We can be either hedonists or citizens, Rousseau insists, not both. The burden of proof is on those who think we can become both.

Taken all in all, Jean-Jacques Rousseau provides us with a

sense of a world coming into being, as well as a world fading away. We recognize the former, its tentative delineations in Rousseau's time congealed into the social formations of our own, as the world in which we, for better and for worse, locate our own being. I conclude this meditation on Rousseau with a historian's characterization of this process of mutual, and sobering, recognition:

> The old hierarchical society of numerous exclusive corporations, of neighbourhood and kin, is disintegrating, and in its place is arising, on the one hand the small nuclear family, and on the other, the omnicompetent State. Rousseau glimpsed both worlds, the world of the *Nouvelle Heloise* and the world of the *Contrat social*. Are they, as Jean-Jacques saw them, mutually exclusive, or are they compatible and complementary? We may answer, perhaps, by looking at ourselves. Do we not live, uneasily, in these two worlds, finding our fulfilment in our intimate circle, and owing a vague, but enforced obligation to the great collectivity, with nothing much in the way of allegiance to anything between? And is not this why the bonds of neighbourhood, community, trade, and vocation are so weak among us, and why the quality of our social life declines even as its material content improves—and why, except for the few who are closest to us and the medical technologists, we die alone?[51]

Notes

1. Relevant titles by Rousseau include *On the Origin of Language*, trans. J. Moran and A. Gode (New York: Frederick Unger, 1966); *Emile*, trans. Allan Bloom (New York: Basic Books, 1979); *The Confessions*, trans. J. N. Cohen (Baltimore: Penguin Books, 1954); *The Government of Poland*, trans. Wilmoore Kendall (Indianapolis: Bobbs-Merrill, 1972); *The First and Second Discourses*, trans. Roger and Judith Masters (New York: St. Martin's Press, 1964); *On the Social Contract, with Geneva Manuscript and Political Economy*, trans. Judith Masters (New York: St. Martin's Press, 1978).

2. See Jean Bethke Elshtain, *Public Man, Private Woman*, (Princeton: Princeton University Press, 1981), pp. 148–70. Curiously, for one who concentrated at times so obsessively on the topic, Rousseau ignores both women and family in his most abstractly legalistic treatise, *The Social Contract*.

3. Rousseau, *Second Discourse*, p. 114.

4. Actually, Rousseau did not give animals the credit they deserve. There is much less instinct in the sense of strictly patterned, signal-oriented behavior among the "beasts," and much more learning and ratiocination, than previously thought. That most people continue to see

beasts as irrational, themselves as reasoning, shows the depth of our immersion in this rationalist prejudice.

5. Rousseau, *Emile*, Book V.

6. See Rousseau, *Social Contract*, p. 170.

7. In this Rousseau resembles many feminist and female thinkers,
from Jane Addams to Margaret Mead.

8. Joel Schwartz, *The Sexual Politics of Jean-Jacques Rousseau*
(Chicago: University of Chicago Press, 1984), came to my attention only
after this chapter was written. He makes essentially the same point in his
text (p. 93).

9. Rousseau, *Emile*, p. 324.

10. Mary Wollstonecraft, *A Vindication of the Rights of Women*, (New
York: W. W. Norton, 1967), p. 75.

11. Ibid., p. 284. Interestingly, Wollstonecraft shares many of the rationalist condemnations of women as flighty, emotional creatures, insisting, of course, that they have been made so by society.

12. Again, take note of the fact that humans can go against that
which the body "naturally" dictates.

13. Rousseau, *Second Discourse*, p. 188.

14. Rousseau, *Emile*, p. 153. A common observation among mothers
is how difficult it is to get their infants to "eat meat," something we were
told was necessary to their health. Hopefully, today's young mothers know
this is not the case.

15. Ibid. Much the same point is made by Gandhi and other pacifist
reformers.

16. Rousseau, *Second Discourse*, p. 109. The shift to animal protein
in the industrial West is implicated in various ecological imbalances as
well, according to environmentalists. A "lay person's" version of this story
may be found in Frances Moore Lappé, *Diet for a Small Planet* (New York:
Ballantine, Friends of the Earth Book, 1971).

17. Rousseau, notes to *Second Discourse*, p. 195

18. Ibid., p. 201.

19. Ibid., p. 199.

20. Wendell Berry, *The Unsettling of America: Culture and Agriculture* (New York: Avon, 1977), p. 104.

21. Rousseau, notes to *Second Discourse*, p. 196. Rousseau's scorn
would be unbounded in light of our nuclearized capacity to destroy.

22. James Miller, *Rousseau: Dreamer of Democracy* (New Haven:
Yale University Press, 1984).

23. See my discussion of Rousseau and the political imagination in
Public Man, Private Woman, pp. 166–68.

24. Rousseau, *Confessions*, p. 328.

25. Rousseau, *Essay on the Origin of Languages*, p. 12.

26. The interested reader is invited to turn to *Public Man, Private
Woman* (pp. 108–27) for a more rounded out discussion of Hobbes and
Locke on language.

27. See, for example, his discussion in the *First Discourse*, p. 42.

28. Recall, for example, Rousseau's insistence that with the creation of the family as a social form the human species enjoyed a great leap in sensibility.

29. See Tony Tanner. "Julie and 'La Maison Paternelle': Another Look at Rousseau's *La Nouvelle Heloise*," in *The Family in Political Thought*, ed. Jean Bethke Elshtain (Amherst, Mass.: University of Massachusetts Press, 1982), pp. 96–124.

30. John McManners, *Death and the Enlightenment: Changing Attitudes to Death Among Christians and Unbelievers in Eighteenth Century France* (Oxford: Clarendon Press, 1981), p. 452.

31. Ibid., p. 453.

32. Robert Darnton, "The Origins of Modern Reading," *The New Republic*, February 27, 1984, pp. 26–33.

33. Ibid., p. 31.

34. Ibid.

35. Wollstonecraft, *Vindication of Rights of Women*, p. 79.

36. Ibid., p. 83.

37. Ibid., p. 146.

38. See Ernst Cassirer, *The Question of Jean-Jacques Rousseau*, trans. Peter Gay (Bloomington: Indiana University Press, 1967), pp. 52–53.

39. Rousseau, *Social Contract*, vols. 1 and 4, pp. 52–53.

40. Rousseau, *Government of Poland*, p. 19.

41. Families can be a threat to civic order and unity, Rousseau observes. But one cannot do without these particular loyalties. An even greater peril lies in trying to eliminate them.

42. Hannah Arendt, *On Revolution* (New York: Penguin Books, 1977), p. 76. To the extent she finds him responsible for articulating the theory behind Robespierre's notion of virtue and the terror it spawned, Arendt is highly critical of Rousseau.

43. Rousseau, *Emile*, note, p. 38.

44. Rousseau, *Government of Poland*, p. 87.

45. Rousseau, *Emile*, p. 40.

46. Rousseau, *Second Discourse*, p. 89.

47. Rousseau, *Government of Poland*, p. 18.

48. Rousseau, *First Discourse*, p. 55. Christianity is incompatible with civic virtue, argues Rousseau, because it divides loyalties, dilutes the general will, and makes men weak. A "society of true Christians would no longer be a society of men" (*Social Contract*, p. 128).

49. Whether, in fact, civic virtue is possible where citizens are not prepared to fight and die for their country is a perennial vexation in political thought. Chapter 8 below takes up the question of war and political discourse explicitly.

50. Wollstonecraft, *Vindication*, p. 43.

51. McManners, *Death and the Enlightenment*, p. 464. I argued, in contradistinction to McManners at one point, that Rousseau, in part of his writing, does find the polity and intimate family compatible and complementary, but he has to go through considerable explicit strain to make them so.

5

Feminism and Citizenship: Liberalism and Its Discontents

> We come into the world alone . . . we leave it alone, under circumstances peculiar to ourselves.
>
> *Elizabeth Cady Stanton*

We live within a world dominated by liberal ideas and ideals. To us they are as self-evident as the truths with which the authors of the Declaration of Independence presented their case against British rule. The self-evident nature of the terms that structure our political universe often makes its points of demarcation difficult to see, even more difficult to get outside of in order to understand, perhaps to criticize, ourselves and our world.[1]

When we describe America as a "liberal society," for example, each of us has some rough notion of what that means. We think of "freedom," first and foremost, of individual right and choice. We also think perhaps of a commitment to fairness, most often defined as equality of opportunity. A bracing sense of 'self' dominates this vision—a human being free to create his and, feminists insist, her own destiny. Feminism from its inception has been a conversation structured by liberalism.[2] A variety of feminisms have emerged to endorse or to challenge this dominant political discourse. Feminism's relation to liberalism historically has been ambivalent, drawing upon some of its features and criticizing others.

Although the form of liberalism that triumphed in American society is strongly individualist, older communitarian and civic republican ideals of the sort espoused by Rousseau were not altogether superseded. We find evocations of collective identity and shared purpose surfacing in some forms of feminist and democratic thinking, past and present. Thus, feminism as a political doctrine and practice is as complex and divided as the larger historic and discursive contexts within which it is lodged. Feminism reflects tensions between individualism and the common good, between rights and sociality, between romantic visions and rationalist orderings, between equality and difference, between the bureaucratic, state-dominated liberalism of the present moment and more radical democratic understandings of politics and citizenship.

I shall take up, first, notions of liberal individualism that continue to dominate our thinking. Although liberalism is a historic formation having multiple expressions in the history of Western societies, my focus will be primarily on its terms of appearance in America. Alexis de Tocqueville's alternately optimistic and mordant pronouncements figure importantly in this portion of the discussion. With tensions between individualist and communitarian construals of the 'self' and politics in mind, I then move to three exemplary feminist thinkers of the nineteenth century showing how each resolved, or failed to resolve, liberalism's conundrums.[3]

Liberal Traditions

What is the theory of self and society that underwrites liberalism? One potent understanding, lying at the basis of much important contemporary political philosophy, is the Kantian argument for the transcendental subject I examined in detail in Chapter 3.[4] The Kantian notion of the self or transcendental subject is bound up with a politics governed by principles that, presuming the priority of right, regulate the ways in which citizens pursue their ends. Right cannot be sacrificed to any ideal of a common good or to some overarching vision of social justice, whether utilitarian ("the greatest good for the greatest number") or Marxist (the communist vision of complete harmony and the transcendence of politics).

Liberalism which begins with this notion of the subject is officially indifferent to the ways of life any single individual chooses to pursue—unless his actions harm someone else. Holding as self-evident a view of the person as a bearer of inalienable rights who must be free to determine his own ends, liberal society promulgates and protects "negative freedom." The citizen is free *from* a public morality he may not share, and free as well from the intrusions of his neighbors into his private affairs. Thomas Jefferson's pronouncement that it mattered not to him whether his neighbor believed in twenty gods or no god—it neither picked his pocket nor broke his leg— captures this liberal ethos well. If I am threatened, I may call upon civil society to protect me just as I may, if necessary, challenge that society if it threatens the priority of right its procedures are duty-bound to sustain. This bracing ideal holds that politics touches externals, individual actions, but cannot guarantee any *particular* vision of social good or collective purpose.

That is one part of the story. Another theoretical strand, coming together to forge modern liberal society, is our inherited notion of a social contract. The contract model has its roots in seventeenth-century social contract theory and it incorporates a vision of society as constituted *by* individuals *for* the fulfillment of individual ends.[5] "The term is also applied," writes Charles Taylor, "to contemporary doctrines which hark back to social contract theory, or which try to defend in some sense the priority of the individual and his rights over society, or which present a purely instrumental view of society." The central feature of this tradition is an "affirmation of what we could call the primacy of rights."[6]

What makes this doctrine of primacy plausible is a commitment to a vision of human self-sufficiency: men as free and independent by nature. Such beings enter into civil society to secure their inalienable rights, which include, in the classical Lockean formulation, the right to life, liberty, and "estates" or property. Thus the strand of liberalism traceable from English social contract theorists forsakes the exalted non-instrumental purity of the Kantian ideal, structuring not just procedures but positing some rough and ready notion of social ends as the concatenation of individual choices. The view that makes freedom an absolute "exalts choice as a human capacity. It carries with it the demand that we become beings capable of choice, that we rise to the level of self-consciousness and autonomy where we can exercise choice, that we not remain enmired through fear, sloth, ignorance, or superstition in some code imposed by tradition, society, or fate which tells us how we should dispose of what belongs to us."[7] Solidifed by later market images of consumer choice, liberal primacy of rights and exaltation of the untrammeled, choosing self triumphed in American constitutional law and popular ideology.

But this triumph was, from its inception, riddled with ambivalence, fraught with unresolved tensions and unconfronted perplexities. Take, briefly, the problem of individual choices and social commitments. In theory, all unchosen constraints are unacceptable: the liberal self must give free consent in order to become the subject of a commitment, legal or moral. But human beings do not enter the world as rational agents capable of consent; rather, we are wholly dependent, vulnerable infants. Where do children, or the family, or other constitutive relations we inherit by birth fit in the liberal scheme of things? Are all our obligations to be construed as the independently chosen aims of an essentially unattached self? Can we truly sustain a notion of our selves as universal, con-textualless, and "unencumbered" in the way liberal theory de-mands?[8] From liberalism's inception a chorus of powerful critics has answered in the negative, or raised serious doubts, even as the attractiveness and forcefulness of liberal ideals is acknowledged.

From Civic Virtue to Competing Interests: Tocqueville's *Democracy in America*

Thousands of words have been spilled analyzing Tocqueville's classic, *Democracy in America*.[9] I turn to Tocqueville briefly not in order to buttress or debate various interpretations but to cap-ture the lineaments of his assessment of nineteenth-century America's political promise and predicaments. It is *this* America that gave rise to a self-conscious feminist movement and to con-trasting forms of feminist theorizing. To see feminism as an at-tempt to "complete the promise of American democracy," or to make our social practices more consistent with our explicit politi-cal professions, is just part of the story. More important is the pos-sibility that liberal principles alone cannot sustain liberal democracy; that, in fact, our way of life ongoingly depends and has depended upon the survival of ties of community and obligation unacknowledged, even suspect, within the dominant ideology.

It was never the intent of the founders to create a classical republic along Rousseauian lines for, argued James Madison in *Federalist 10*, mankind can never attain "perfect equality" whether in "political rights . . . possessions, their opinions, and their pas-sions."[10] For Madison, social homogeneity is both undesirable and impossible; "natural distinctions" are invariably augmented by "ar-tificial ones." Rather than simply lamenting this fact, or, perhaps, seeking to eliminate distinctions altogether, one must provide for the more or less orderly working out of compulsions to distinguish and to divide.

Rousseau's republics of civic virtue are impossible to achieve in practice because they require of individuals the ability to tran-scend competing interests in the name of some common good. Per-

haps, in previous epochs, human beings living within small, homogenous societies could attain or approximate an ideal of civic
virtue. But the modern world has unleashed forces, individual and
collective, that undercut such older ideals: a world driven by interest, dedicated to commerce, and heterogenous as societies in-
termingle through trade and populations migrate—these and more
are incompatible with the discipline, restraint, and education to
citizenship demanded of Rousseau's virtuous, independent farmer-
citizens and their chaste wives.

Tocqueville, however, resists junking the classic civic republican vision altogether. Why? Because the empirical reality of
American democracy, in his view, even as it frees individuals from
the constraints of older, undemocratic structures and obligations
also unleashes atomism, individualism, privatization. His fear is
not that this invites anarchy; rather, he believes that "the atomized
individualism of an acquisitive bourgeois society will engender oppressive new forms of social and political domination."[11] Individual disassociation invites the tyranny of mass opinion and
centralized political authority. The lure of private acquisitiveness
spawns political apathy and invites democratic despotism. Isolated
and impotent, all social webs that once held persons intact having
disintegrated, the individual finds himself exposed and un-
protected. Into this power vacuum moves "the organizing force of
the government," the centralized state.[12]

This is pretty bleak stuff. But Tocqueville also insisted that
American democracy had the means to avoid this fate, to respond
to atomization and disassociation. He found the cure to social
democracy in political liberty—in the plethora of voluntary political and beneficent associations in which Americans participated
as well as in structured guarantees of genuine power at municipal
and state levels. His is an early vision of participatory democracy
in which the 'moment' of civic virtue is sustained in loose and diverse forms in a variety of associations pursuing multiple, not singular, ends. Participation that begins as mere self-interest may be
transformed as "democratic man becomes more than *mere* bourgeois: he becomes, in part and on occasion, a genuinely public-
spirited republican citizen as well."[13]

Nineteenth-century America, captured by Tocqueville, is a society whose ideals breed simultaneous strengths and weaknesses.
A new world, freed from the orthodox and corporate constraints of
the old, American democracy would either fulfill its bracing promise of liberty with equality or sink in a surfeit of privatized, individualistic apathy accompanied by an unchecked momentum to-

ward centralization and ultimate despotism. His political hope rested in a society honeycombed by multiple, voluntary political associations, check-mating tendencies toward coercive homogeneity. The centralized state must be curbed and limited just as social atomization must be muted and mediated through the coming together of citizens for self-interested *and* public-spirited ends.

Feminism and the American Liberal Tradition

American feminism historically presents an admixture of potent elements—primacy of rights liberalism and procedural constitutionalism, a celebration of the woman as autonomous 'self'—these features of classical liberalism commingle with calls to social harmony and community and celebrations of women as the repositories *par excellence* of civic virtue, the rightful arbiters of social norms and the guardians of private and, ultimately, public morality.[14]

Liberalism has been attractive to feminist thinkers. Its stated presuppositions and rhetoric serve as a potent wedge for reform. The language of rights applies a powerful corrosive to taken-for-granted obligations, particularly those of family duty or any social status declared "natural" on the basis of "ascriptive characteristics." (Thus denial of suffrage to women; denial of freedom to black slaves; denial of equal protection under the law to categories of workers, etc., all came under critical scrutiny given liberalism's commitment to freedom and equality.) To be "free" and "equal" as men are became a central aim of feminist reform. The political strategy that followed was one of inclusion and incorporation: women, too, were rational beings. It followed that women, too were bearers of inalienable rights. It followed that *qua* woman, there was no valid basis to exclude women as a group from the burdens and benefits of equal citizenship. All men and women are created equal: thus the 1848 "Declaration of Sentiments" at Seneca Falls.

The nineteenth-century feminism exemplified in the women's suffrage movement can best be understood within the framework of an "equal rights" formulation. Spokeswomen for the suffrage movement were celebrants of legal equality who acted to undermine arguments which justified formal legalistic inequality on grounds of sex differences. Equal rights feminists claimed that denying a group of persons basic rights on the grounds of some presumed difference cannot be justified unless it can be shown that the difference is relevant to the distinction being made. Whatever differences might exist between the sexes—none justifies legal inequality and denial of the rights and privileges of citizenship.

But most suffragists were not liberal absolutists. They did not push liberal universalism to its most radical conclusion—that there are no justifiable bases for exclusion of adult human beings from legal equality and citizenship. For suffragists were also heirs of a tradition that stressed the need for social order and shared values, emphasizing civic education, a Protestant civic religion, and the importance of having a propertied stake in society. Thus the demand made at the Seneca Falls Convention for the "immediate admission to all rights and privileges which belong to them [women] as citizens of the United States," was never intended to apply to *all* women.[15] Leading suffragists believed there were some differences that justified inequality in citizenship rights and privileges on the grounds of "relevant" distinctions.

For Elizabeth Cady Stanton, for example, illiteracy constituted a sufficient criterion for denial of the franchise. This meant, of course, that many women would be denied the right to vote—but as illiterates, not as women. Others favored exclusion of both males and females of certain immigrant groups. Southern suffragists and their supporters proclaimed the vote for white Southern women as a force to "offset" the influence of newly enfranchised black males. In the struggle over suffrage, feminism appropriated selectively features of liberal inclusiveness and republican exclusiveness.

At times, feminism's gerrymandered discourse turned liberal egalitarianism on its head—arguing *for* women's civic equality on grounds, particularly motherhood, that served historically to guarantee women's exclusion from politics. Thus one finds the case for greater female political participation being lodged on the ground of women's moral supremacy and characteristic forms of virtue. Such appeals, strategic though they may have been, were never *merely* strategic. They spoke to and from women's social location as mothers, using motherhood as a claim to citizenship and to public identity. They reflected centuries of women's culture. At various times, radical, liberal, democratic, and socialist feminists have paid homage to women as exemplars of particular forms of social virtue.

From the vantage point of contemporary individualism and rights-based feminism, emphases on "republican motherhood" were a trap and a delusion, an attempt to find virtue in oppressive necessity. But this is far too simple and arrogantly present-minded. The discourse that evoked images of maternal virtue was a response to a very complex, rapidly changing political culture. That political culture was committed to liberalism and, as well, incorporated republican themes of social solidarity and national identity. Women made their case within a male-dominant political order from *their* own sphere, a world of female-structured sensibility and imperatives that signified doubly their exclusion from political life and their cultural strength and importance.

Poised on the edge of Tocqueville's democratic dream/nightmare, feminists variously pushed integral, individualist liberalism and "equality with difference." Less able than men to embrace an identity as a wholly autonomous social atom, often rejecting explicitly the individualist ideal as refracted through commercial acquisitive values, many of these daughters of American democracy endorsed familial or communal values to counter hyperindividualism and to promote *solidarisme*.[16]

Feminist and female-dominated reform movements also turned to Christian notions of self and community to soften possessive individualism. The utopian socialist, Charles Fourier, gained a favorable hearing in some quarters because of his paeon to human "brotherhood" and because his portrait of a cooperative community evoked Christian visions of the "peaceable kingdom." Communalists often raised questions about the operation of free-market capitalism, pointing to the human flotsam and jetsam it created and the unsavory, cut-throat competition that served as its motor.[17]

Carroll Smith-Rosenberg has described one 'civic virtue' reform effort, the New York Female Moral Reform Society. This group predates the Declaration of Sentiments by more than a decade and reflects much of the moralistic fervor of female-based social reform that construed the citizen in terms beyond those of suffrage or formal equality. The major target of the Female Moral Reform Society was sexual abuse, including prostitution, and this abuse was laid directly at the doorstep of deformations in male sexuality. "They proposed," writes Rosenberg, "through their organization to extirpate sexual license and the double standard from American society."[18] Stressing a vision of the moralized community rather than individual rights, the Female Moral Reform Society denounced "the lascivious and predatory nature of the American Male" even as they called for a national women's union to forge a new social order.[19] They stressed sisterhood and female solidarity, finding in a specifically feminized Christian ethos the only true hope for a new world—in Rosenberg's words a "feminine-sororial community which might help break down...isolation, lighten the monotony and harshness of life, and establish a counter-system of female values and priorities."[20]

Three Feminist Thinkers

More must be added to this already heady brew. If one dominant motif of feminist and feminized reform found in sexual passion a source of social disorder, there were self-described feminists
who were unabashed romantics. The most notable is Margaret
Fuller, writer, transcendentalist, and intellectual colleague of
Emerson and Thoreau. In 1844 she published her famous essay,
Woman in the Nineteenth Century, which articulates a super-
charged celebration of male-female divergence as archetypal forms.
For Fuller, women are different from men and deserve equal rights
and opportunities in order to assert their unique qualities. William
L. O'Neill draws attention to Fuller's vigor in attacking the "binding conventions of her day," but argues that she denigrated her
own intellectual capacities as a philosopher by falling back on
"transcendental cliches" about the nature of woman.[21] But this
critique comes from the standpoint of one who applauds the rationalist version of feminism. Fuller's arguments may be "transcendental" but it does not follow that they are trite. Without relying
on the familiar standbys—God, the Bible, motherhood—she articulated intensely-felt notions of woman's "especial genius."

In addition to favoring the emancipation of women from "ar-
tificial" restrictions and retrograde laws, Fuller called for each
woman's emancipation from her own subjective prison. She perceived, before psychoanalytic language was available for this purpose, that *repression* as well as *oppression* were problems for
women. This perception led to her emphasis on instinct and intuition and her desire for the "soul to live freely and unimpeded."[22]
Her emphasis on repression differs from the predominant concern
with objective conditions. Most feminists, when they mentioned
Fuller, cited her independent life as exemplary rather than her
thoughts, for it was more directly within the vein of liberal constitutionalism to couch one's protest on the basis of individual right
than on the grounds that the "electrical, the magnetic element in
Woman" had not been fairly emphasized.[23] The feminine aspect,
Fuller rhapsodizes, "the side of love, of beauty, of holiness," is also
found in men of genius and sensitivity—the poet Shelley is a case
in point. Because the growth of humankind embraces such complementary dualities as "Energy and Harmony; Power and Beauty;
Intellect and Love," it is both masculine and feminine.[24]

Finding masculinity and feminity not pure, linear constructs
but qualities toward which one tends more or less, she rejects the
notion of strict sex-role differentiation—not in the name of liberal
equality but of poetry, genius, intuition. Woman's soul is shared

with that of man, but modified in her as a woman, "...it flows, it breathes, it sings...[that] which is especially feminine flushes in blossom the face of the earth, and pervades like air and water all this seeming solid globe, daily renewing and purifying its life. Such may be the especially feminine element spoken of as Femality. But it is no more the order of nature that it should be incarnated pure in any form, than that the masculine energy should exist unmingled with it in any form."[25] Both masculine and feminine powers, in Fuller's vision, tend toward Platonic perfection and efflorescent fullness of a vaguely defined natural sort.

Fuller does make contact with the dominant motif of feminist thought—the notion of an autonomous self. What she does not do is set the dominant male up as the standard of what is to count as a rational, free being. Indeed, she believes it is the prisonhouse of bad institutions that compels the woman to emulate a man if she wishes to be free. Restricted in her effort to develop those qualities that are uniquely her own, she becomes a reflection of those she perceives to be more free. If she is to have a dignity, a woman must stand alone. Only then can she achieve her own perfection and the free development of her soul. Only then will there be "unison in variety, congeniality in differences."[26] Fuller's romanticism represents a minority position subordinate to the forces of rational egalitarianism, although the always eclectic Elizabeth Cady Stanton cited both Fuller and John Stuart Mill, reflecting the ambivalence in her own position.

Cady Stanton is a fascinating thinker in large part because she espoused, at different points in her long career, aspects of the liberal, civic republican, scientific, and nativist worldviews.[27] Stanton sought both freedom *from* the state and freedom *through* the state. She promulgated the free market yet argued for community. Like Jane Addams later, she admired the Italian republican nationalism of Guiseppe Mazzini but she also endorsed the strong liberal individualism of John Stuart Mill. William Leach has discussed in detail Stanton's admiration of positivist philosophers, including eugenicists and others we now look upon as less than savory. For example: "she proposed as early as 1870 that the state should prevent the marriage of the morally, physically, and mentally unfit."[28] She was not beyond openly racist arguments—perhaps nativist would be the better term—attacking "unlettered and unwashed ditch-diggers, boot-blacks, butchers, and barbers" and demanding to know how women (of the better sort) remained unfranchised when "Sambo, Patrick, Hans and Yung Fung" were not.[29] She spoke about "the human family" and, in one of her most famous speeches, "the solitude of self." This mix of tension-filled elements should not be construed as Stanton's confusion; rather, it reflects the diverse and not wholly compatible jumble of ideas that make up American political and social life and thought in her era.

Stanton's espousal of positive freedom comes through loud and clear. Suffrage is a right. But it is also a means by which women's potentialities can be developed. She kept a sense of realism about suffrage—unlike some of her enthusiastic compatriots—recognizing that the "ballot in the hand of woman will bring neither the millennium nor pandemonium the next day; but it will surely right many wrongs."[30] She also proposed a restructuring of American society away from what she saw as a too confining nuclear family toward some sort of communal or cooperative arrangement. Her opposition to the nuclear family stemmed in part from her belief that a woman's mind is degraded from constant contact with children and servants. The isolation of the household restricts and cramps her aspirations and cuts her off from the active flow of life; moreover, many parents, she insisted, "are not fit to have control of children, hence the State should see that they are sheltered, fed, clothed, and educated. It is far better for the State to make good citizens of its children in the beginning, than, in the end, to be compelled to care for them as criminals."[31] Her concern with republican motherhood comes through in her celebration of the "scientific" theory of *Mütterrecht* or "mother-right" associated with the anthropological speculations of Bachofen. Convinced by his arguments, and those of another armchair anthropologist, Lewis Morgan, that the origin of society lay with a matriarchate, Stanton credits "the instincts of motherhood" with the creation of social life and deems "the wisdom and tender sentiments growing out of motherhood" the "greatest civilizing power."[32]

If pressed to locate Stanton in *a* tradition of discourse, however, the ethical doctrine of the liberal self would come closest to the heart of her theorizing. In 1894 she penned an essay, which she cites in her autobiography, in which she insists that the "true standpoint from which to view this question [marriage and maternity] is individual sovereignty, individual happiness. It is often said that the interests of society are paramount, and first to be considered. This was the Roman idea, the Pagan idea, that the individual was made for the State. The central idea of barbarism has ever been the family, the tribe, the nation—never the individual. But the great doctrine of Christianity is the right of individual conscience and judgement."[33] Building on this foundation, she had earlier noted the "solitude of self," a beautifully written speech that is, at one and the same time, exhilarating and chilling in its relentless insistence on the self-alone.

The individuial is preeminent, first and foremost, Stanton argues strongly, deploying the Robinson Crusoe metaphor to characterize women on their solitary islands. After the self comes citizenship, then the generic woman, and the last the "incidental relations of life, such as mother, wife, sister, daughter...."[34] These incidental relations are not constitutive of self. Stanton's self, in line with classical liberal evocations, is evoked as prior to social arrangements. She speaks of the "self-sovereignty" of women and men and calls human beings solitary voyagers. We come into the world alone. We go out alone. We "walk alone." We realize our "awful solitude." When things go well, others cluster around; when they go badly there is "not one to share her misery...." Life is a "march" and a "battle" and we are all soldiers who must be "equipped" for our own "protection." Women require rights, therefore, and legal equality to protect themselves in their solitary march, to gird themselves for battle. In "the tragedies and triumphs of human experience, each mortal stands alone."[35] Yet, as if to take some of the edge off this razor-sharp evocation of self-alone, she calls, as does Mill, for "complete individual development for the general good."[36]

Stanton's words are chilling because they conjure up a universe alternately hostile or benignly indifferent—depopulated save for the self. The universe has been stripped of meaning save what the individual gives to it and its objects. She aims to disenthrall the self, to disencumber it in the sure and certain hope that a lofty and invigorating ideal of freedom will be the end result—and redound to the general good. This locates Stanton squarely in the strongest version of the liberal ideal. It also raises some disquieting questions, primarily about whether we can regard "ourselves as independent in this way without great costs to those loyalties and convictions whose moral force consists partly in the fact that living by them is inseparable from understanding ourselves as the particular persons we are...."[37]

Charlotte Perkins Gilman is a third important feminist theorist who struggled with the vagaries of the liberal tradition. Her major theoretical work, *Women and Economics*, appeared in 1898. A biting exposition on the relationship between the sexes couched in the popular sociological and evolutionary theorizing of the day, Gilman hitches the cause of women to the trajectory of history, proclaiming history on the side of women who seek to restructure economic and social relations. She assumes that human evolution proceeds on an inevitable, natural, uniform course: a linear movement toward ultimate perfection (or nearly so)—an apogee that requires scientific knowledge and rational control over events.

Economic relations are the most important factor in the evolution of the species, according to Gilman, and woman's loss of economic independence means she has failed to keep pace on the evolutionary scale. The association of the sex relation with economic relations is, therefore, a "frightful source of evils."[38] Although at one point in time the "sexuo-economic relation" made sense, at present it results in an excessive sex-attraction that invites, in turn, a morbid preoccupation (on the part of women) with sexual attractiveness as well as intense selfishness. To Gilman, sex relations must be defused and stripped of their lingering romantic patina—reduced to what is necessary for reproduction and rationalized. If economic dependence is removed, the sex drive will once again function in its proper evolutionary perspective—simply to maintain the species.

If environment changes, human qualities change: one aspect of Gilman's work is a belief in the extreme malleability of the human species. Yet she also speculates on possible innate differences between the sexes. She believes the sexes exhibit certain physical attributions. The tendency to fight is generally masculine, but the tendency to "protect and provide for, is a sex-distinction of females in general."[39] Man's unhealthy and excessive sex-distinctions, such as his bellicose nature, has been moderated in the course of history and put at the service of progress. But women's sex-linked distinctions are overdeveloped because of her economic dependence, cutting women off "from the direct action of natural selection."[40]

Gilman's solution fuses elements of liberal individualism, communalism, and, above all, the science of society. The household, child-rearing, and food preparation must be collectivized and put on a scientific basis. "Human progress lies in the perfecting of the social organization," she writes.[41] Child-rearing, for example, if it were rationalized and no longer dependent on the whims, foibles, and ignorance of individual mothers, will result in healthier, happier, more intelligent children. This change, and others, can take place within existing society on a "business-like basis." She proposes that urban dwelling places for professional women with families consist of large apartment buildings incorporating a common dining room, a kitchen staffed by professionals, a roof-garden, day nurseries and kindergartens also staffed by professionals, and a cadre of cleaners and sanitation workers hired by management: the rationalized life.

The point of this rationalized collective society is to free the individual and Gilman sees no apparent conflict between her twin imperatives. Although she deplores the rampant, unchecked, individualistic capitalism of her day and desires collectivization of much industry, she continues to argue that the highest good for women lies in individualism. An advocate of social planning and engineering, Gilman anticipates much of the enthusiasm for a science of society that entered in full force in the Progressive Era. Leach sees in "the great rationalist-socialist work of Charlotte Perkins Gilman" the dual commitment to individualism and liberal capitalism, together with a transformed view of community, that derailed the feminist project in important ways. For even Gilman "viewed the market place almost uncritically and could say of the nineteenth-century male that he 'was so far the only fully human being'."[42] Gilman's schemes all call for control by elites and experts, a rationalization Leach is correct to find "ultimately antilibertarian," despite continued paeons to individual freedom.

The writings of these vital and diverse feminist thinkers illustrate deeper strands and tensions that continue to vex contemporary American political life and thought. Is it possible to sustain strong communities without losing the value of the individual? Can we evoke a robust concept of the citizen, and his or her obligations to the state, while retaining freedom *from* state intrusion? These are the questions that seem never to go away, nor should they.[43]

Notes

1. This interpretive dilemma refers back to the epistemological debates noted in Chapter 1.

2. This is true of Marxist feminisms as well, for Marxism makes necessary reference to the liberal *Weltanschauung*. As Barbara Taylor notes in *Eve and the New Jerusalem* (New York: Pantheon Books, 1983), "The ideological roots of Socialist feminism lay in the popular democratic tradition of the late eighteenth century . . ." (p. 1). She cites Wollstonecraft's rationalist liberalism as an important forerunner to later doctrines.

3. I go over contemporary feminisms in detail in *Public Man, Private Woman* (Princeton: Princeton University Press, 1981) and refer the interested reader to Chapter 5 of that work.

4. John Rawls's influential *A Theory of Justice* (Cambridge: Harvard University Press, 1972), is explicitly Kantian in its presuppositions and commitments.

5. Thomas Hobbes, *Leviathan*, ed. Michael Oakeshott (New York: Collier Books, 1966), and John Locke, *Two Treatises of Government*, ed. Peter Laslett (New York: New American Library, 1965), are the two key texts. Hobbes and Locke differ from one another, often dramatically, but each can be drawn upon to support notions of an "individual" as given, antecedent to a social order. See the discussion in Elshtain, *Public Man, Private Woman*, pp. 108–27. Hobbes and Locke are criticized by Rousseau from his very different starting point in his notes to the *Second Discourse*.

6. Charles Taylor, "Atomism," in *Power, Possessions and Freedom: Essays in Honor of C. B. Macpherson*, ed. Alkis Kantos (Toronto: University of Toronto Press, 1979), pp. 39–61, 48.

7. Ibid.

8. The "unencumbered self" is Michael Sandel's term, drawn from his essay "The Procedural Republic and the Unencumbered Self," *Political Theory* 12 (February 1984):81–96.

9. Alexis de Tocqueville, *Democracy in America*, ed. Phillips Bradley (New York: Vintage, 1945), 2 vols.

10. *The Federalist*, ed. Benjamin F. Wright (Cambridge: Harvard University Press, 1961), p. 133.

11. Richard W. Krouse, "Classical Images of Democracy in America: Madison and Tocqueville," in *Democratic Theory and Practice*, ed. Graeme Duncan (Cambridge: Cambridge University Press, 1973), pp. 58–78.

12. Tocqueville, *Democracy in America*, vol. 1, p. 340.

13. Krouse, "Classical Images of Democracy," p. 74.

14. I shall not consider at length Marxism's challenge to liberalism for several reasons. First, Marx's theories do not figure importantly in the story of classical American liberalism, the American environment proving inhospitable to orthodox Marxist formulations. Second, social movements of the nineteenth century in which "women's emancipation" figured centrally belong within the "utopian" strand of socialist thinking, a strand to which Marx and Marxism were antagonistic. If this were a book on social movements rather than social and political thought, the lacunae here noted would be more problematic. See Taylor, *Eve and the New Jerusalem* to help fill the gap.

15. Elizabeth Cady Stanton, Susan B. Anthony, Matilda Joslyn Gage, eds., *History of Woman Suffrage*, vol. 1 (Rochester, N.Y.: Charles Mann, 1881), p. 71.

16. See the discussion by Karen Offen, "Depopulation, Nationalism, and Feminism in Fin-de-Siecle France," *The American Historical Review* 89 (June 1984):648–76 for a cross-cultural treatment of these themes.

17. Most often these did not usher into anything like systematic, full-fledged critiques, remaining underdeveloped intimations. Even self-described socialists, like Charlotte Perkins Gilman, had good words for the market.

18. Carroll Smith-Rosenberg, "Beauty, the Beast, and the Militant Woman," in Nancy F. Cott and Elizabeth H. Pleck, *A Heritage of Her Own* (New York: Touchstone Book, 1979), pp. 197–221, 201.

19. Ibid., p. 204

20. Ibid., pp. 209–10. The entire Cott, Pleck collection is a rich source of social history and thought. Also recommended, Aileen S. Kraditor, *Up From the Pedestal: Selected Writings in the History of American Feminism* (Chicago: Quadrangle Books, 1968).

21. William L. O'Neill, *Everyone Was Brave: The Rise and Fall of Feminism in America* (Chicago: Quadrangle Books, 1969), pp. 8–9.

22. Mason Wade, ed., *The Writings of Margaret Fuller* (New York: Viking Press, 1941), p. 125.

23. Ibid., p. 168.

24. Ibid., p. 211.

25. Ibid., p. 176.

26. Ibid., p. 137.

27. Rogers Smith, in " 'One United People' Discriminatory Citizenship Laws and the American Quest for Community, 1800–1937" (Yale University: ms., 1983), has identified liberalism, republicanism, and nativism as "distinguishable sets of ideas or traditions of discourse" within American life. I have added scientism to this list, though it plays off the other three in complex ways.

28. William Leach, *True Love and Perfect Union* (New York: Basic Books, 1980), p. 151.

29. Stanton et al., *History of Woman Suffrage*, vol. 1, pp. 270, 354.

30. Elizabeth Cady Stanton, Susan B. Anthony, and Matilda Joslyn Gage, eds. *History of Woman Suffrage*, vol. 2 (Rochester, N.Y.: Charles Mann, 1886), p. 307.

31. Elizabeth Cady Stanton, *Eighty Years and More: Reminiscences 1815–1897* (New York: Schocken Books, 1971), pp. 429–430.

32. Elizabeth Cady Stanton, "The Matriarchate," excerpted in Kraditor, *Up From the Pedestal*, pp. 140–147, 143.

33. Stanton, *Eighty Years and More*, p. 231.

34. Elizabeth Cady Stanton, *Solitude of Self* (Kailua, Hawaii: published privately by Doris M. Ladd and Jane Wilkins Pultz, 1979), p. 1.

35. Stanton, *Solitude of Self*, pp. 2, 4, 9.

36. Ibid., p. 3.

37. Michael J. Sandel, *Liberalism and the Limits of Justice* (Cambridge: Cambridge University Press, 1982), p. 179.

38. Charlotte Perkins Gilman, *Women and Economics* (New York: Harper Torchbook, 1966), p. 26.

39. Ibid., p. 41.

40. Ibid., p. 70. As genetics this makes little sense, of course, but Gilman is arguing from a point of sociological evolution.

41. Ibid., p. 162.

42. Leach, *True Love and Perfect Union*, p. 348.

43. I return to the question of the contemporary democratic citizen in my concluding chapter.

6

Self/Other, Citizen/State:
G. W. F. Hegel and Jane Addams

> I was convinced that disinterested action was like truth or beauty
> in its lucidity and power of appeal.
>
> *Jane Addams*

Jane Addams is a familiar name to students of American history. Though her once great fame has faded, we continue to learn of "Jane Addams of Hull House" and the era of Progressive reform of which she was a leading exemplar. But few scholars pay much attention to Addams as a social and political theorist.[1] The name "Hegel," on the other hand, conjures up the intimidating picture of a world-historic thinker, a philosopher whose works are synonymous with grand, imposing systematicity. Yet Hegel and Addams meet on the ground of shared concerns—at least that is the argument I shall make. If we look at some of the problems each thinker was trying to solve, or a few of the questions by which each was vexed in turn, startling similarities emerge.

Hegel writes of "family, civil society, and the state"; Jane Addams of "the family claim" and the "social claim." Both struggled with the nature and purpose of the state and the relation of the human being, as "self" and "citizen," to the public world. From the point of view of a materialist, Hegel and Addams are idealists. From the point of view of an abstract idealist metaphysic, however, Addams and Hegel are lodged in embodiment and social reality. Neither fits tidily with the liberal tradition, broadly defined, though Hegel's project makes necessary reference to Kant and Addam's to American liberal culture in and through its exemplary texts and political figures. But there is an important difference in how each

71

has been received and appropriated: Hegel is rightly celebrated as a theoretical giant. But Addams, though she was given her day as an activist, has yet to receive her due as a thinker.

Taking the measure of Hegel and Addams's responses to the historic forces at work in their respective epochs, including the coming into existence of the centralized nation-state and modern nationalism, helps us to think about men, women, and the state in our own era.

Hegel and Our Age

It is impossible to approach anything like completeness in a brief discussion of Hegel. I shall stay with the central lineaments of his theory. Hegel's 'self' emerges in a particular historic situation and this self reflects—or has the power to reflect—on that situation. Self-knowledge must always be cast in historical form. Experience must be earned, in a sense, and made one's own. Self-identity is ongoing and changes over time. At any given moment we as human subjects both are and are not. We simultaneously affirm and negate if we are open to the battle of reason and to the ambiguous disclosures of lived life. Thinking proceeds through negation, through a complex dynamic that enables us to absorb particular, concrete reality into a more systematic and complete formulation and understanding.

This no doubt says both too little and too much: too little for those who already have at least passing familiarity with Hegel and too much for those for whom he is obscure and unknown. But it must do for now. One point that should be stressed is that Hegel's is no passive account of mind and knowledge. He challenges the presumptions of common sense empiricists or, in our day, simple behaviorists who believe understanding proceeds from, and rests upon, observable facts and brute data. If facts do not exist "as such" for Hegel neither does the human subject or self. His is a complex depiction of the human subject's capacity for consciousness and self-consciousness as the mind works actively and purposively upon material given to it through the senses.[2]

The salient features of Hegel's social thought, for the purpose of this discussion, revolve around the three moments or aspects of ethical life, *Sittlichkeit*, in Hegel's system. These are the family, ethical life in its natural or immediate phase; civil society, ethical life in its division and appearance; and the state, the sphere of universal ethical life and freedom.[3] It is with his understanding of the inner meaning, or content, of each of these spheres that Hegel articulates a complex vision and structures dilemmas that later thinkers have had to contend with in their own reflections on liberal civil society, private life, and the state.

In contrast to classical liberalism, Hegel refuses to reduce either the family or the sphere of the state to the point of contract. His repudiation of contract theories of marriage is explicit. In the complex dialectic of love, one finds one's 'self' only through absorption in the 'other'. The individual is not unchanged with the unfolding of this ethical moment. The family is not a series of exchanges between pre-posited social atoms but a many-faceted social form that fulfills basic human needs—for sustenance, for sexuality, for intimacy—irreducible to the sum of these commingled parts. One cannot capture the family as a sphere of ethical life under any description that takes one part (say, sexuality, or the legal contract that inaugurates marriage) for the whole thing.

Within the natural ethical realm of the family, women are in their preeminent domain. Women are the ethically particular beings *par excellence*. The "law of the family is her inherent implicit inward nature," Hegel writes.[4] Concerned with the philosophical meaning of family and love, Hegel finds the family necessary for its reciprocal identifications, its unity based on feeling, and as a kind of civic training ground: Rousseau's republican mother hovers in the background. The relations of the sphere of ethical particularity are required, indeed they make possible, civic identity and solidarity with the wider community ("itself an individuality")—at least for the male who alone is a citizen.

While the family as a moral ideal and social reality (however imperfectly realized in Hegel's sense) cannot from itself guarantee the emergence of autonomous moral agents, or individuals with a commitment to freedom, reflective self-understanding, and citizenship, such developed human qualities cannot flourish in societies, real or theorized, in which 'the family' as moral ideal and social reality has been eliminated or has disintegrated.

Hegel would find support for his argument in the histories of twentieth-century totalitarian societies. Modern absolutist states without exception have taken various steps to eradicate the family as an autonomous social sphere, a locus for identity, and an arena of concrete loyalties. From Plato's plans to abolish 'private families' for his Guardian class (in the interest of making the city as 'one'), to the relentless policies of the Nazi German state designed to shred private loyalties and to turn the family into just another cog in the wheel of the Reich, thinkers and political leaders who demand total loyalty and who fear plurality, multiplicity of associations, and diversity of purposes *must* destroy families and must eradicate 'the family' in Hegel's sense. Families are sources of meaning, purpose, and commitment at least somewhat outside the dominant order and ideology.

On this issue Hegel's discussion is notable for its richness and complexity. But there are irritants in the image if one works from a perspective informed by Jane Addams's concern for an active civic life *for* women. Hegel dubs womankind "the everlasting irony [in the life] of the community." Woman, he argues, changes "by intrigue the universal end of government into a private end, transforms its universal activity into a work of some particular individual, and perverts the universal property of the state into a possession and ornament for the Family."[5] Women are petty-minded, in his view, and corrosive of a wider universal purpose and spirit. The woman is too individualistic, too predatory in behalf of her own. The individualism Hegel condemns here is not synonymous with the abstract individualism of classical liberalism but represents, instead, a familial insularity. She attains vicarious victories (Hegel suggests) through the "power of youth," her son. But it is a pyrrhic victory for the "brave youth in whom woman finds her pleasure...now has his day and his worth is openly acknowledged"—in War.

Family insularity, the heavy hand of Mother, may impede the young man's transition to citizenship by goading him into premature individualism within civil society. The only "cure" for a disease liberal society itself ongoingly creates by bringing into being both the *necessary* particularity of the family and that sphere of triumphant self-interest, bourgeois civil society, is the state and the state's most potent medicine is War. Otherwise one finds only familial particularity and atomized contractualism. These two alone or taken together are insufficient to ground freedom and universal ethical life.[6]

As sketched this sounds rather nasty, and certainly my highly condensed version does not do justice to Hegel's complete argument. Hegel is trying to get at dynamics he finds at work in the modern world. That world is complicatedly at odds with itself but in ways that contain possibilities for resolution. For example: we require families. Without these relations life would be Hobbes's nasty, brutish, and short nightmare. But families insure separatism, division into independent entities "presided over by womankind." For civilization to triumph, for the sphere of reason to enlarge its reign, the family must be interfered with and individual self-consciousness dissolved. Woman is thus essential and yet "an internal enemy," a view similar to points in Rousseau and to several of Freud's remarks in *Civilization and its Discontents*. Necessary to—but not an essential part of—that is the irony of woman's situation as Hegel sketches it.[7]

Hegel's is a grand vision of the state. It is, to recall Aristotle's characterization of the *polis*, the "final and perfect association"—in Hegelian language the "actuality of the ethical idea." As a state-identified being, I am fulfilled only so long as I live through my communion with other citizens. My freedom is dependent on that of others, hence a supercession of the rapacious and individualistic freedom of civil society. The state transcends both familial insularity and the competitive anomie of civil society. The dynamic of civil society is an incessant machine, in Hegel's view, that transforms human needs and creates expectations it cannot, from itself, satisfy. It is a cauldron unceasingly producing conflicts, dehumanization, and disparities of wealth and poverty.

Enter the state and a way, first, to meet the human needs left unsatisfied by the competitive individualism of civil society and, second, to transcend the conflict endemic to that sphere. The state is that arena that calls upon and sustains the individual's commitment to universal ethical life, satisfying these yearnings through sacrifice in "behalf of the individuality of the state...."[8] For with the state comes not simply the possibility but the inevitability of war. The human work of courage plays itself out in "the genuine, absolute, final end, the sovereignty of the state."[9] The modern world guarantees this end by transforming personal bravery into something impersonal, for "thought has invented the gun, and the invention of this weapon, which has changed the purely personal form of bravery into a more abstract one, is no accident."[10]

War transcends material values. The individual reaches for a common end. Solidarity and the power of association find a sphere of action. This solidarity is immanent within the state form. But it, and the nation, come to life with war. Peace poses the specific danger of sanctioning the view that the atomized world of society is absolute.[11] In war, however, the state as a collective being is tested and, as well, the citizen recognizes the state as the source of all rights. Just as the individual emerges to self-conscious identity only through a struggle, so the state must struggle to attain recognition. The state's proclamation of its own sovereignty is not enough—that sovereignty must be recognized just as the individual, to be a 'self', must be recognized by an 'other'. War is the means to attain recognition, to pass, in a sense, the definitive test of political manhood.[12]

As well, war is a reminder of the finiteness of individual existence. The awesome power of negativity, of death, makes itself manifest as we are drawn out of ourselves into a larger purpose. Of course, men and women are drawn out differently. The woman gives up her son. The man becomes what he in some sense is *meant* to be by being absorbed in the larger stream of life—war and the state.[13] In all this, Hegel does not glorify war. But he declares it a necessity, insisting it plays, and has played, vital historic functions. He prods us to ask why people, men and women, seem to like war so much—even as they hate it. Perhaps one reason men and women often recall wartime with fondness is for the reasons Hegel notes: they are a part of something larger than themselves: they are absorbed more fully in a communal, not simply an individualistic, freedom. They play their part in an effort that requires solidarity with their fellows. Life seems larger, somehow, and even more precious because it is threatened. This is a reverberating theme in memories and memoirs of war.[14]

The lure of war—its embodiment of the state in a grand sense; its assurance of group cohesion—forms one of the intractable poles in the life and work of Jane Addams. Addams emerges in a heady time in American life, politically and intellectually. To call her, as most do, a Pragmatist after the manner of John Dewey is accurate but incomplete. Addams and Dewey drew upon a complex background that included Hegel's philosophy as transmitted and Americanized in the work of Josiah Royce, who stressed the social bases of self and morality, and George Herbert Mead, the greatest American theorist of self/other.

Mead's Hegelianized argument holds that the self cannot arise outside social experience, nor exist in independence from an other.[15] Mead insisted, with Hegel, that consciousness of one's own self-consciousness needs recognition by others to exist. But we are not so *entirely* dependent on the social group in its relation to the self (Mead's word for the social whole is the "generalized other") that we must be swept up automatically, or nearly so, in group enthusiasms. Mead offers some space for an individual to brave the disapproval of the generalized other by setting up "a higher sort of community which in a certain sense outvotes the one we find," thus having a voice which "is more than the voice of the community."[16]

Mead's account of ethical life finds a sphere of reason and freedom beyond the state—indeed higher than the state—a community of conscience. It is this moralized vision of a yet-to-be-realized community that helps us to understand Addams's social thought and to interpret the diverse ways in which she struggled with the problems Hegel unearthed so cannily—the ethical duty to family but its limited particularity; the corrosive effect of civil society on social relations and community, yet its role in historicizing and transforming needs and springing individuals loose from particular ties; and the modern state and our identification *with* its universally cast purposes. How, then, does Jane Addams resolve the struggles of self/other and citizen/state in her social theory?

A Return to Hull House: Jane Addams and Social Thought

Mistrusting systematic, highly abstract theory, understanding how such thinking invites dogmatism, Jane Addams's approach to thought bears little resemblance to the grand Hegelian edifice. Addams's is a story-shaped life constituted in and through narrative. Her favorite mode of expression was autobiography. But she shares with Hegel the conviction that the self cannot define itself outside complex social relations. Rather than grasping these truths through overpowering language and logic, Addams begins with empathy and experience. She agrees with Rousseau: one starts with feeling. To truly understand *any* individual or feature of social life, one must enter sympathetically into the self-understanding of the other and of ways of being different from one's own. Her essays, speeches, and longer autobiographical accounts revolve around stories: she generalizes universal imperatives from thickly described particular dilemmas and events.

The world in which young Jane Addams grew up was a world in transition. Dominated by the rise of the market, and the radically transforming forces of capitalist accumulation, older primary relations of family and clan, small town and village, came under what was to be decades of relentless pressure. Urban centers grew up and out of control. Thousands of immigrants flooded into cities unprepared to deal with this influx of humanity. Crime, poverty, illness, unsanitary conditions, unemployment, prostitution: the image of a pastoral democracy became a Jeffersonian dream of the past. Hegel, of course, had marked the nature of civil society well. And he had attempted to work out dialectically interrelated but separate spheres of influence, including the family and the state as well as the realm of *homo economicus*. But women, in and through all of this, remained the "everlasting irony."

For Jane Addams, one of the first generation of college women, the world presented a picture not so much of inescapable irony as, to her mind, transformable dependencies and interdependencies. Her solution to the Hegelian dilemma of the woman in the home was neither to keep her there, an everlasting irony in the community, nor to spring her wholesale into the competitiveness of civil society, but to transform the woman into a civic being, leading an active life as one who acknowledges both "the family claim" and "the social claim" and complexly mediates the legitimate obligations and possibilities flowing from each.

In her essay, "Filial Relations," which appeared in the collection, *Democracy and Social Ethics*, Addams described the conflict between familial duties and dependencies and the responsibilities of the individual to the larger social whole as one both necessary and tragic. "The collision of interests, each of which has a real moral basis and a right to its own place in life, is bound to be more or less tragic. It is the struggle between two claims, the destruction of either of which would bring ruin to ethical life."[17] Hegel would not disagree. But Addams and Hegel part company on how these respective moments of ethical life, each with its "right to its own place in life" can best be preserved—can be held in some fructifying tension with one another rather than becoming paralyzing and destructive to individuals and, thereby, corrosive of the social good.

Addams understood, as Hegel did not, that women could not ongoingly play out the drama of ethical life in the private sphere of the family alone. Eventually the structure will collapse—even within Hegel's terms this seems likely. Just as the public world predominates and gives meaning to the private, for Hegel public identity is central. In serving the state, the man serves a purpose larger than his own life, yet one which is the ground of his identity. But surely it is not only males whose identities are tied to the public world if we take seriously Hegel's insistence that language is essential to a shared way of life and that public and private experiences and imperatives are in some sense linguistically structured.[18] Man becomes alienated if public experiences are drained of meaning. But such alienation must be woman's lot as well, at least in part, because even if women cannot act *within* the public world, they can act, or believe they are acting for, or *in the interests of* that world—sending off sons to die in war is one grim example.

The corrosive effects of civil society cannot be forestalled indefinitely. Addams understood this and she understood as well that, deprived of direct responsibility to and for the state, women were less capable of imparting a capacity for civic virtue to others—to their children. Addams raises to an explicit concern questions of female identity and political purpose—the conflicts in which Hegel's women find themselves irrevocably stuck, unable to do other than what they have always done. Women, too, must undergo a struggle for identity and self-consciousness. They, too, must wrestle with dependencies and enter a wider realm of action—if they are to sustain the civic order and to serve the cause of freedom. That, at least, is Addams's hard-won conclusion. Although she asserted the "ultimate supremacy of moral agencies," she linked these to a reflective female awareness.[19] Women—the sister as well as Hegel's "brother"—experiences a need to be "useful" and a part of life's larger adventure. Never wavering from the conviction that women were different from men, and had a particular sensibility to offer to the greater good, Addams called upon women to enter the world yet not to abandon their own emotional and ethical lives. The family claim *is* a claim: we are duty-bound to answer. But it is not the only claim and cannot absorb the whole of us.

To truly enter into ethical life, Addams argues, one must resist grand claims couched in universal abstractions and bring matters down to earth. Life is a moral quest, she declares, and a life of virtue lies within the reach of all: hers is a moral egalitarianism that feeds democratic commitments. Addams insists that we not "kick off" the particular as we reach for universal understandings or imperatives. To keep one's feet on the ground, she proposes a secular version of the 'imitatio Christi'. For example: she charted her own life by measuring herself up against "Mr. Lincoln," a figure with whom she self-consciously identified.

Addams describes moral life and existence by filtering it *through* particular individuals and relations. For truth "may be discovered by honest reminiscence."[20] No social abstraction has authenticity, she argued, unless it is rooted in concrete human experience. Her immersion in the particular, her ability to articulate wider social meaning through powerful depictions of individual suffering or joy, hope or despair, sets her apart from those who write abstractly about moral life. One example will illustrate the suffering the early wage-labor system trailed in its wake. Addams pens an unforgettable word portrait of a single suffering woman, one human story beneath—or beyond—Hegel's theoretical characterizations of the sphere of civil society and the poor it necessarily (in Hegel's view) creates:

With all the efforts made by modern society to nurture and educate the young, how stupid it is to permit the mothers of young
children to spend themselves in the coarser work of the world!
It is curiously inconsistent that with the emphasis this generation has placed upon the mother and upon the prolongation of
infancy, we constantly allow the waste of this most precious material. I cannot recall without indignation a recent experience. I
was detained late one evening in an office building by a prolonged
committee meeting of the Board of Education. As I came out at
eleven o'clock I met in the corridor of the fourteenth floor a
woman whom I knew, on her knees scrubbing the marble tiling.
As she straightened to greet me, she seemed so wet from her feet
up to her chin, that I hastily inquired the cause. Her reply was
that she left home at five o'clock every night and had no opportunity for six hours to nurse her baby. Her mother's milk mingled with the very water with which she scrubbed the floors until she should return at midnight, heated and exhausted, to feed
her screaming child with what remained within her breasts.[21]

This is very powerful stuff—a potent anthropological description meant to arouse moral feeling, to call forth compassion. Addams was convinced that only a tug upon our human sympathies
and affections can draw us into an ethical life and keep us
there—in contrast to Kantian categorical imperatives and Hegelian
systematizing—and her stories exemplify this belief. "Pity, memory, and faithfulness are natural ties with paramount claims," she
writes."[22] But in this vignette we see those claims—the "family
claim"—run over roughshod by the requirements of an economi-
cally rapacious, socially irresponsible order. The scrubwoman is
the actuality of family claim and the wider social claim. And her
situation, Addams assures us, is not unique but representative of
the life of the immigrant poor.

Endorsing a life of action, articulating a social ontology that
was Christian in its origins and tilt toward the poor and downtrod-
den, Addams became a state enthusiast. Although she insisted
upon the need for individual effort, she joined other reformers in
looking to the state as an embodiment of a social ethic of care, and
as a way to ameliorate the dislocations produced by bourgeois civil
society. That she was overoptimistic in her commitment to the
beneficent state is no doubt true. With other Progressives she was
a meliorist who sought adjustment to the new industrial order and
its inevitable alienations. But she and the state came to a tragic
parting of the ways and this break highlights her most dramatic
disassociation from Hegel's political thought.

The rupture for Addams is World War I. Hegel's theory of war, remember, is of an activity limited in its aims and means, a uniting struggle for recognition calling citizens into a shared effort. War in this mold is the agent of reason and freedom. For Addams such talk is an errant capitulation to murder, an embrace of the state as a terrible engine of death. For one who had long associated herself with the buoyant certainty that the world was slowly but surely progressing toward ever more inclusive and benign forms—toward international cooperation, interdependence, and peace, "an inevitable historical advance," the war was a terrible blow. Breaking with such Progressive colleagues as John Dewey, who reconciled themselves to the war, Addams insisted that war coarsened human relations and posed a threat, in the short and long runs, to democratic institutions. Hegel's solidarity is bought, for Addams, at too high a price.

She writes: ". . . some of us had suspected that social advance depends as much upon the process through which it is secured as upon the result itself. . . ."[23] Of course, she was stirred by the self-sacrificing response of youth, by their patriotism and sense of duty. Courage and a sense of devotion are always admirable. But surely we can enlist these enthusiasms in some grand cause that does not involve killing or being killed? Disillusioned by the transformation of the state into an engine of war, Addams's ideal of the democratic state as an avatar of justice collapsed. She continued to hope the state could be turned to benign purposes. But she never took up—in any cogent way—Hegel's challenge that unity of state purpose is not possible in a liberal, individualist society unless the nation is at war.

Speaking from the point of view of "woman," defined not as an everlasting irony but as the sorrowing mother of the dislocated and dead, Addams evoked images of women as creators of non-statist social forms. In a passage that would only confirm Hegel's view of women as mired in the particular, Addams writes: "Undoubtedly women were then told that the interests of the tribe, the diminishing food supply, the honor of the chieftain, demanded that they leave their particular caves and go out in the wind and weather without regard to the survival of their children. But at the present moment the very names of the tribes and of the honors and the glories which they sought are forgotten, while the basic fact that the mothers held the lives of their children above all else, insisted upon staying where the children had a chance to live, and cultivate the earth for their food, laid the foundations of an ordered society."[24]

In celebrations of selfless male action in wartime, Addams sees a centuries-old trail of tears. She also alerts us to how difficult it is to stand against the "generalized other," the state-at-war, for one is "starved of any gratification of that natural desire to have [his own] decisions justified by his fellows."[25] To combat war enthusiasms, for Hegel was right about the solidarity they require and inspire, identity with a non-statist ethic is needed. Addams found it in a civil religion indebted to Protestant Christianity and in a network of activists, most of them women, some of them pacifists. Family, civil society, and the state, she insists, do not suffice as bases for ethical life. One also requires communities of conscience, associations and movements, many plural possibilities. Otherwise, especially in times of social upheaval, the state will be all that remains standing and we will be compelled to love it—as Simone Weil once chillingly wrote—because nothing else exists.

During her lifetime, Jane Addams saw the state in which she reposed such high ethical hopes become a calculating engine of mass slaughter.[26] She did not go as far in her disillusioned critique as Randolph Bourne, another member of the Progressive intelligentsia, but never again could she entertain high Hegelian hopes. For Bourne's devastating refrain, in his unfinished 1919 fragment on the state, "War is the health of the state," though a vulgarization, comes harrowingly close to Hegel's theory of war and the state. Writes Bourne: "Citizens are no longer indifferent to their Government, but each cell of the body politic is brimming with life and activity. We are at last on the way to full realization of that collective community in which each individual somehow contains the virtue of the whole. In a nation at war, every citizen identifies himself with the whole, and feels immensely strengthened in that identification."[27] It is this certainty that represents, for Hegel, a vital, necessary moment of ethical life. But Jane Addams sees civic tragedy, the reaffirmation of force, and the crushing of lives and hope. Between these two positions there can be no resolution.[28]

Notes

1. Christopher Lasch is an important exception. He discusses Addams at length in his *New Radicalism in America, 1889–1963* (New York: Vintage, 1965), pp. 3–37 and in his edited collection of excerpts from her writings, published as *The Social Thought of Jane Addams* (Indianapolis: Bobbs-Merrill, 1965). Jane Addams was born in 1860; she died in 1935.

2. For this discussion I draw upon Hegel, *Phenomenology of Spirit*, trans. A. V. Miller (London: Oxford University Press, 1977), as well as on

my previous interpretations in *Public Man, Private Woman* (Princeton: Princeton University Press, 1981). G. W. F. Hegel's life spans the tumultuous years 1770–1831.

3. The key Hegel text here is *Philosophy of Right*, trans. T. M. Knox (London: Oxford University Press, 1967). A highly condensed and lucid advanced introduction to Hegel's understanding of ethical life and theory of the state remains Shlomo Avineri, *Hegel's Theory of the Modern State* (Cambridge: Cambridge University Press, 1972).

4. Hegel, *Phenomenology*, p. 476. Cf. paragraph of *Philosophy of Right*, pp. 114–15.

5. Hegel, *Phenomenology*, p. 488.

6. This should sound familiar if one remembers Tocqueville's apprehensions concerning the characteristic vice toward which bourgeois civil society pushes—social fragmentation, the breakdown of association, and so on.

7. See also Hegel's discussion of Antigone in *Phenomenology* and *Philosophy of Right* and contrast it with Jean Bethke Elshtain, "Antigone's Daughters," *Democracy* (April 1982):46–59.

8. Hegel, *Philosophy of Right*, p. 210.

9. Ibid., p. 211.

10. Ibid., p. 212.

11. See Hegel, *Philosophy of Right*, p. 278.

12. If one surveys briefly just the wars fought in the post World War II era, most have been wars of "national liberation," wars to create and to gain recognition for one's nation. Hegel would certainly see this as evidence for his thesis.

13. Avineri's chapter on "War" in *Hegel's Theory of the Modern State* is provocative and detailed.

14. Hegel does warn that protracted war may backfire, may have debilitating effects, as does any war that is total rather than limited, fueled by rapaciousness rather than the struggle for recognition.

15. George Herbert Mead, *Mind, Self and Society* (Chicago: University of Chicago Press, 1962), p. 140.

16. Ibid., pp. 167–68, 189.

17. Jane Addams, *Democracy and Social Ethics* (New York: Macmillan, 1902), pp. 76–77.

18. I draw here upon portions of the discussion of Hegel in *Public Man, Private Woman*, p. 180.

19. Jane Addams, *The Long Road of Woman's Memory* (New York: Macmillan, 1916), p. 129.

20. Jane Addams, *Second Twenty Years at Hull House* in *Forty Years at Hull House* (New York: Macmillan, 1935), p. 6.

21. Jane Addams, *Twenty Years at Hull House* (New York: Macmillan, 1968), pp. 174–75.

22. Ibid., p. 247.

23. Jane Addams, *Peace and Bread in Time of War* (Boston: G. K. Hall, 1960), p. 132.

24. Addams, *Long Road*, pp. 126–27.

25. Addams, *Peace and Bread*, p. 150.

26. For example, in the first day of the Battle of the Somme, July 1, 1916, 110,000 British men got out of the trenches and began to walk forward along a thirteen-mile front. They had no visible enemy to fight; they wore number tags around their necks; 60,000 were dead by the end of the day. This is the modern soldier not as a warrior but as cannon fodder, an observation Addams made over and over again of the tragedy of World War I.

27. Randolph Bourne, *The Radical Will, 1911–1918* (New York: Urizen, 1978), p. 361.

28. Perhaps, horrifyingly, the possibility of nuclear war literally explodes Hegel's theory of war. For nuclear war cannot end in mutual state-recognitions but, instead, in mutual state obliterations, thus defeating the major purpose of war-fighting. As well, because nuclear war is total and indiscriminate it does not allow for solidarity and commitment; rather, as social atoms, we are all potential victims and there are no warriors.

7

Freud and the Therapeutic Society: *Homo Politicus* or *Homo Psychologicus?*

For it is not so easy to play upon the instrument of the soul.
Sigmund Freud

Freud's is a magesterial but ambivalent legacy. He has been treated as a great political thinker, one who rightfully belongs in the canon of the Western tradition, and he has also been characterized as subversive of that tradition. Both views are correct. Freud's work is so vast and so complex that it admits of multiple interpretations and has spawned dozens of competing schools. In the words of W. H. Auden, Freud is no longer a thinker but a "whole climate of opinion." Which directions—politically—does that climate of opinion push? I will take up a number of possibilities, treating Freud not in a great books manner, which presumes a self-contained discourse selected and solidified over time, but in light of the visions of the human being and human social life his theories call forth and help to sustain. A subtext running through my discussion, surfacing explicitly at points, is the way psychoanalytic theory constitutes the subject and his or her civic capacities (or incapacities) specifically.

Order, authority, the range and scope of freedom, limiting conditions to social change—these are among the inescapable questions of political thought and Freud treats each of these perennial vexations. He ranges over much of the same turf as a Hobbes or a Rousseau. But Freud's solutions, to the extent he proffers them, do not lie in the creation of a transformed public life but in gearing the human subject to accept *necessity* even as he or she struggles for a limited *freedom* and a modicum of *justice*. Freud warned against the creation of a vast *Weltanschauung*, "an intellectual construction which solves all the problems of our existence uniformly on the basis of one overriding hypothesis, which, accordingly, leaves no question unanswered and in which everything that interests us finds its fixed place. It will easily be understood that the possession of a *Weltanschauung* of this kind is among the ideal wishes of human beings."[1] Theoretical grandiosity of the systemic and formal sort, Freud argues at points, invites or can be drawn upon to legitimate totalistic political orders that squeeze out space for human diversity in meeting the specifications of a foreordained vision.

Although Freud does not give politics over to the devil, in Luther's sense, he does see politics as a sphere of irrationalism justifying itself self-servingly, disguising the bases of its own order and authority. Resolutely anti-Utopian, hoping, in Carl Schorske's words, to make "bearable a political world spun out of orbit and beyond control," Freud emerges as our greatest modern Stoic.[2] Yet Freud has been located as a thinker whose thought provides the rich mulch out of which utopian gardens grow—including those of the feminist variety. I shall take up the ways in which Freud's discourse empties concepts of political meaning, substituting instead psychological content. Female imagery figures subtly in the first section, explicitly in later portions of the chapter.

Psychoanalysis and *Homo Politicus*

The developmental psychologist, Jerome Bruner, has suggested that Freud's revolution in our understanding of the human subject is an idea, or complex of ideas, of public scope and import. He writes: "Since the idea of man is of the order of *res publica*, it is an idea not subject to change without public debate."[3] By *res publica* Bruner refers off-handedly to that which is publicly available or in the air. We children of Freud, he suggests, all possess or have access to "the idea of man" he promulgated so powerfully and so successfully. True. We think of the human being as *homo sexualis* above all.

But Bruner's statement is puzzling nevertheless for there was no "public debate" of the sort one usually thinks of when one conjures up political struggle as our governing view of human beings shifted toward the psychological pole. Instead, psychoanalytic construals became a driving force in a transformed order of discourse, thought, and ways of being. This was preceded by no discussion among citizens; indeed, the combined forces that help to bring such shifts into being are not manifestly available and open to transparent review and explicit debate.

A more interesting question is whether in fact psychoanalytic theory *is* a theory of the 'common good' or 'civic virtue' or can serve as the foundation for such. If one understands *res publica* is a sense different from Bruner's simple reduction to "that which is public or available," the question becomes more problematic. An understanding drawn from political thought, and tied to the particular subject matter of its discourse, sees *res publica* as that which is the shared property of a people: a specific, delimited field for human action in which human beings are constituted as citizens. The fact of one's generic humanness does not suffice to constitute the human subject as a political being. To become such another identity, remembering Rousseau, is required: a civic identity, the subject as *homo politicus*.

Psychoanalytic theory is double-edged on the question of its subject. On the one hand, Freud articulated a poignant, radically egalitarian view of human beings.[4] Freud's Everyman—and Woman—is a being who cannot escape necessity and in whom desire has agentic force. As conceived by Freud, psychoanalysis is preeminently a theory of the psychodynamic self, the night traveler who wakes in wonder or in terror, the rational irrationalist, the romantic hero or heroine, the vulnerable child, the builder, the destroyer, the giver, the taker, the authoritarian, the anarchist, attempting to carve out a liveable life in history between the intractable pole of necessity and the ephemeral dream of possibility. There is an expressive subject, importantly self-defining and active, no mere social 'product', who inhabits his pages. It is this subject psychoanalytic discourse helps to constitute and it is this subject who interprets and is interpreted.[5] What psychoanalysis is best equipped to do—given its subject—is to probe meanings, individual and social. The 'social' is understood in various ways by Freud: sometimes as an aggregate concatenation of individual meanings, a convergence; sometimes as that which is thinkable given an overarching system of meta-meanings, the cultural superego. The psychoanalytic self is a knowing self who, out of transformed knowledge, can alter in part the terms of his or her self-identity.[6]

This is powerful stuff but what has it to do with the politics or with political man and woman? It is possible to trace out connections. A human being in the grip of a neurosis is a privatized be-

ing spinning his or her wheels in an interiorized world, cut-off from
effective action in and on the world. To break the neurosis is to become at once more public, more social. Freud would add: to become more autonomous, to be capable of standing *against* the
compact majority, for Freud's political injunctions are cast nega-
tively. The political implications and import of such moral autonomy is important: to the extent that individuals are self-defining
in the way Freud advocates they can more readily resist tyranni-
cal and manipulative public power. But note that we are talking
of *individuals*—that the ground of being is a radically solitary one.
In order to sustain the analytic attitude of constant vigilance, criticism, self-criticism, the individual cannot be absorbed *within* a
movement or political community or transported by an idea that
takes one out of 'the self'.

Freud's subject demands much of the self, including a complex
plumbing of motivation. Here things get tricky. There is more at
stake for Freud than inward governance or Kant's good will. Nor
is the psychoanalytic self a Kantian being severed into a noumenal,
free aspect and a phenomenal, determined appearance. We are instead beings driven by complex, embodied desires, laced through
and through with ideas, expressed within language. As well, psychoanalytic therapy proceeds from, or within, a human social relationship in which love must play a part or no transformation can
occur. Often called "the talking cure," psychoanalysis is at least
as much (in Freud's terms) the "cure through love." So Freud's
subject is no solipsist. But there is a way in which the psychoanalytic self is a richly private being who views all that is public with
a skeptical eye; who is resolutely disillusioned about politics; who
is implacably opposed to a collective search for, or involvement in,
transcendent purposes and meanings.

I suggested a double-edge to the psychoanalytic subject. The
first, mentioned briefly above, is the Everyman or Everywoman
whose humanity is shared with the entire species, who is born, has
needs and desires, suffers, experiences moments of joy, finally dies.
This trans-historically concrete level is terribly abstract. The ab-
stractness of such a univeral lies in the fact that we really don't
know what to make of our shared humanness other than a general
attitude of beneficence and, perhaps, humility.[7] In this sense,
Freud is one of the great theorists of an *inclusive* view of humanity.

But politics in the modern world necessarily *divides* us, showing us as particular and exclusive. Another way to put it might be:
politics makes manifest our divisions and offers a positive way to
treat them. We are divided by national identification, by race, sex,

class, ethnicity, religion, and so on. In politics, we treat such divisions in complex ways as we try to forge unities, and reach commonalities, out of diversities without quashing diversity in the process.[8] Freud's theory grounds us as beings whose commonality is *not* a potential achievement, wrung from our diversity, but a given. But his version of our generic humanity fails to provide us with a ground for political selfhood or political being. Political identities (national, ethnic, etc.) are seen as a block to wider, more inclusive collectivities.

Freud's theory begins with Everyperson. For a psychological theory tied to therapeutic practice this was in many ways a liberating place to begin. It enabled Freud to see the "normal" self as a "fiction" but a "necessary one" and to tie that self to those then despised as possessed or beneath contempt, beings of a putatively different order from the respectable bourgeois self. By tying the satisfied *burgher* to the suffering hysteric Freud pricked pomposity and promoted generous impulses. But Freud's 'self' loses, or mutes, the claims of action. He or she becomes more social, breaking out of self-defeating, self-replicating patterns, ideally in order to take his or her part in what Philip Rieff has called a "negative community" forged on the basis of an incessantly critical and self-critical analytic spirit.

One arrives at the rarified exclusivity of those who truly breathe the heady, bracing air of subliminated reason—a small company and necessarily so, Freud argued. He harbored no utopian illusions that the whole world would one day consist of the disillusioned. An ongoing struggle would be required even to preserve a spark of critique and sustain the psychoanalytic enterprise in a world bent on destroying all bearers of pessimistic, or grave, tidings.[9]

Psychoanalysis, to Freud, was subversive of the received terms of *any* given scheme of things. For all social orders are built up on illusions psychoanalysis, properly understood, must deconstruct. Every social order is erected on a foundation of guilt, repressions, deceits, illusions. The community with no illusions is Freud's a- or anti-political community of the elect. To be sure, Freud hoped to broaden that community; hoped to find ways to educate children into the analytic spirit or attitude. But, in the meantime, psychoanalysis cannot serve as the ground out of which a public world emerges, nor be the basis for political justifications.

Freud's exclusive community calls to mind Luther's tiny handful of Christians who need no external rule to order things—but the vast majority, not being deep believers, require the prince, God's hangman. A more apt analogy, perhaps, is to classical Stoicism. The Stoics offered a combination of universalism with exclusivity also featured in psychoanalysis and Freud's vision of the psychoanalytic community.[10] Wolin notes the Stoic appeal to "universal values of reason, equality, and freedom," on the one hand, and, on the other, "the strain of intellectual snobbery that tended to restrict membership. . .to an elite. . .a kind of invisible church of rational beings."[11]

For all the richness of Freud's basic texts—the case studies, the metapsychology, the essays on the theory of sexuality, the broader theory of culture—his account of the disillusioned adult self is too thin to sustain a public identity or political and social action and hope. In this Freud represents not an alternative to, but an extension of, specific features of classical liberal conceptions of the self and the wider order.[12] Similarly, the psychoanalytic self, whose *real* existence is in a complex dialogue with the self, is suited to the alienating terms of life in modern bureaucratic statist society.[13] Psychoanalysis fails to account for much that is constitutive of self, features of identity that go beyond the universal features I share with human beings as such as well as the particulars of the oedipal configurations of my (and each person's) infancy and childhood. I refer here to my ties to and with others through shared allegiance to, say, a historic community, a religion, a lingering idea (for example, the Marxist theory of revolution), a place, a kin network, a movement, and so on. Freud's freedom is freedom from neurotic delusion and public illusion.[14]

The disillusioned psychoanalytic self, as a morally autonomous being, enjoys rich social relations with his or her family and friends and has ties to a wider, cosmopolitan community of nonbelievers. But he must fight devotion to a nation, to a religion, or an overarching idea. All of Freud's concerns are valid: they are valid because of the mound of bodies on which the nation-state rests; because of the history of intolerance and injustice perpetrated in the name of religion; because a *Weltanschauung* causes people to believe they are members of a master race. All of Freud's indictments ring true. And yet Freud knew these ties would always beckon and that they could, at best, be chastened, not eliminated. Because he saw only the negative side of the ledger—or concentrated on those features—he refused to affirm any ideal of polity and could see in religion only a form of (infantilized) seeking after security and meaning. But it seems to me that Freud also know that without transcendent illusion the task of culture becomes more and more problematic.

Reflect for a moment on the following: for Freud identification (entering empathically into the lives of others while respecting their individual existence) is the source of the social tie. Human beings are bound together in such a way that they can recognize others as human. They can do this because Eros and Thanatos (Freud's overarching myth of libidinal and aggressive drives, respectively) can be redirected in their aims and much of their energy suffused and diffused within a wider social network. In *Group Psychology and the Analysis of Ego*, Freud details the ways in which horizontal links, inner ties between and among individuals, are made possible *because of* shared identifications with an overarching idea or set of practices or meanings. Shared vertical links to Church, to Army (Freud's examples) alone make possible identification on the horizontal plane. Thus the dynamics of identification completes two tasks, tying individuals *to* one another through their shared identification *with* some-thing in common. Groups are distinguished from one another as a result of the vertical ties they do, and do not, share.[15]

.   Surely there is a paradox here. Freud would deconstruct reigning identifications to institutions and ideas he considers built on illusion, hence regressive, and substitute a vague commitment to the rule of reason. Yet, at the same time, he sees the need to preserve, strengthen, and extend identification to make social life less brutal and unjust. The vertical plane is essential to this process. Some sixty years after *Group Psychology*, and in light of the theory and practice of fascism, Freud's determination to sever the individual and claims of transcendence have great force. The most murderous manifestations of the vertical-horizontal bond in modernity got played out in Nazi terror. Many have drawn disillusioned conclusions from this history and it would be foolish to underplay the power of such arguments.

But perhaps twentieth-century fascism suggests another lesson. Perhaps it tells us that the denial of transcendent possibility, the repression of the romantic, the triumph of scientific rationalism—the disenchantment of the world in Max Weber's apt phrase—makes more likely the eruption of such human imperatives as some monstrous return of the repressed. Freud's rationalist god is cold comfort. Perhaps it is impossible to forge a unity out of diversity without the deep sharing of certain illusions. Perhaps our task is not to destroy *all* illusions and enthusiasms, as Freud's negative community must, but to determine which enable us to reach out to others in bonds of hope and enthusiasm and which derive their energy primarily from an aggressive exclusivity that requires making demons or enemies out of others.[16]

What has this to do with the politics? If neither our shared humanness, nor our membership in a negative, analytic community suffices to forge a political identity—a political attitude, perhaps, but not civic being—how does one reach for the *res publica* in a post-Freudian age? Remember, political identity emerges from a ground that simultaneously divides and unites us. We are unavoidably heirs of a particular tradition; beneficiaries or victims of a particular history; citizens or subjects of a specific political culture. *Political* being involves an act of identification that is, to the extent we appropriate it self-consciously as adults, also an act of faith and an expression of hope. A politics that does not tie us to one another through some ideals we share is a politics in trouble—and that is, in part, the story of contemporary liberal societies.

Liberalism's minimalist or thin notion of politics and political society was accompanied by an accretion of rich notions of the bourgeois subject, an often splendid vision of a nuanced and complex private world. With the reigning notion of politics trimmed down from classical understandings, the modern liberal, as a public being, is enjoined to act in accordance with specified rules and procedures, neither expecting nor demanding too much from the public world. But we seem, at the moment, immersed in excessive proceduralism, hence a politics that less and less grips our imaginations. At the same time, the private world is more and more one of sanctioned consumption and obsessive preoccupation with 'the self'. All points seem to revolve around the individual's subjective feelings—whether of frustration, anxiety, stress, fulfillment. The citizen recedes; the therapeutic subject prevails.[17]

The Therapeutic Society and Its Malcontents

While it would be tendentious to blame Freud for modern therapeutic enthusiasms and compulsions, the plenary jolt he delivered to received understandings further pulled the rug out from under notions of civic identity or being. We must first put our own houses in order. We must see to ourselves. To throw ourselves into whatever identities the public world offers is to, perhaps, gain power and the world's glory but at the price of one's soul (psyche). The psychoanalytic self, like the Jew, must remain a perpetual outsider (Freud linked the two): then and only then can he be true to himself and the project of radical self-understanding and negative social critique.

Politics in our time is displaced and a therapeutic world view, one which constitutes the subject as a client or a patient, as well or ill, as neurotically miserable or happily fulfilled, is part and parcel of a politics of displacement.[18] This is a dynamic that comes into play when certain conditions prevail: (1) Established public and private, secular and religious, institutions and rules are in flux and people have a sense that the center will not hold; (2) There are no clearly established public institutions and ways of acting to focus dissent and hope; (3) Private values, exigencies and identities take precedence over public involvement as a citizen. Such a politics begins and ends with *my* feelings. Private good, recast in therapeutic society as fulfillment or individualized liberation, takes precedence over public identities, values, purposes.

Human beings are frequently enjoined to remake themselves anew in such a society, to strip off the past entirely, and to embrace a politics of the triumphalist person. Collective identity grounded in shared historic experience—problematic, to be sure, for those who have not been the dominant public persons—or forged from mutual involvement in determinate activities and relations aimed at the attainment of public ideals, is ruled out in favor of the embrace of an abstraction: the self as a wholly free being. Only that which is real, immediate, satisfying to 'me' is legitimate. Jeremiads against this therapeutic self are in long supply and alternatives few. But there is one further feature of the depoliticization of the moment that provides a conceptual link to an *inversion* I detect in the psychoanalytic construction of being.

In an interesting essay on "Destructive *Gemeinschaft*," Richard Sennett argues that the present insistence on *gemeinschaft* relations, on authenticity and intensity, is destructive along a number of planes. Important for this discussion is the distorted notion of the public world that flows from immersion in what Sennett calls a "psychomorphic view of society, one in which questions of class, race, and history are all abolished in favor of explanations which turn on the character and motivations of participants in society."[19] We have, Sennett argues, moved from a rich, bourgeois notion of privacy and "the private" (Freud's), which insisted upon reserve, decorum, concealment, which resisted demands to open to the glare of publicity all that made one who one, in private, was, to a publicized notion of "intimacy" that precisely makes such demands. That Freud is seen, by some, as the grandfather of present demands for liberation as the untrammeled unleashing of individual feelings and desires is a vulgar construal. But this vulgarity contains a moment of truth: it has connections to the psychoanalytic concept of repression and the terms of its historic appropriation and embrace.

The family, redefined as an "intrapersonal association" rather than an intergenerational institution, becomes the source of a strange "familialism"—the conviction that intimate experiences and identities are, by definition, political and can and must serve as the foundation for a new political order.[20] The upshot of all this burden of self (for there is no civic order, no political identity, that allows us to face one another as citizens rather than private beings pleading our cases and baring our souls in this form of thinking) is, in Sennett's words, "the tendency to measure the world as a mirror of self." Society, not a polity, matters "only as manifestations of personality and personal feelings...."[21] What one brings to the public world is one's surplus subjectivity. What the public world is there to do is to further promote one's individualized fulfillment: and so on. Nothing could be further from classical construals of a *res publica*. For in this pseudo-therapeutic image, the self treats the public world as a consumer approaches a department store: as having something *for* me, something *I* want.

It would, of course, be ludicrous to blame psychoanalysis for the malaise of the present. But in taking the measure of that malaise it is important to locate psychoanalysis, its medicalization and popularization, as part of a broader cultural understanding. Now to that inversion mentioned above—one implicated in the decline of political possibility. The critique to follow is not of Freud so much as a whole approach to the question of being and action. A political being is and must be one who acts in public on the basis of a civic identity. Any theory that shifts the terms of identity almost wholly away from action toward interior authenticity or noumenal willing severed from the phenomenal act is suspect, in this argument, from the standpoint of polity. Any theory which locates freedom in the self rather than as that action by citizens within a public space is, from the point of view I am developing, suspect.

I take my cue from two texts: Bruno Bettelheim's *The Informed Heart* and Philip Hallie's *Lest Innocent Blood be Shed.*[22] Hallie tells the story of the village of Le Chambon-sur-Lignon and the goodness that happened there during one of this century's darkest moments. A traditional, rural community, sharing a deep religious commitment, committed itself to resist the Nazi terror, to rescue Jews by giving them food, shelter, and asylum at the risk of their own lives, providing them with false identity cards and helping them to escape into neutral Switzerland. This community of pietists determined to act. Decisions that were turning points in the struggle took place in kitchens. Community members later spoke of the "kitchen debates." Inspired by an ethical system that saw looking into one's own soul as inadequate, for one must also assay the good or evil that surrounds one, the villagers of Le Chambon became political in a deadly age. Resistance was inadequate if construed as an act of private dissent or an interior withholding of approval—the tendencies noted in Lutheran doctrine in Chapter 2 above. One didn't plumb one's own motivations or explore them therapeutically—as in psychoanalysis—to see if one was really seeking self-glory, or killing the father, or finding substitutive satisfaction. The villagers had no access to, hence were not defined by, psychotherapeutic language or discourse. They did have access to the family as an ethical institution and they did share a set of beliefs capable of serving as a catalyst for civic identity. After the fact they reflected on the "whys" of what they had done. At the time, there was a clear imperative: one must act to diminish evil in the world. The villagers exemplified civic virtue and the freedom to act it makes possible. The lesson they teach us is *not* a positive one we can directly emulate—Americans do not exist in homogenous, rural villages any longer—but a negative one. That is, we are reminded that any theory that casts a relentlessly suspicious spotlight on action may diminish possibilities for individual and shared commitment by turning the self inward rather than pushing the self into the world.

Bettelheim assesses his experience as a prisoner in the Nazi concentration camp at Dachau with psychoanalytic theory in mind explicitly. Himself a psychoanalyst, Bettelheim claims it was *unimportant* why a person acted as he did in Dachau. The "only thing that counted was how he acted."[23] Bettelheim does not mean to disarticulate altogether the why of action from the how. Instead, he wishes to transform our usual terms of explanation for action. Oversimply, Bettelheim's experience convinced him that *how* a person acts "can alter what he is"—that the lines of determination may flow from action to the 'inner self' rather than exclusively the other direction. One's true self was revealed in one's actions—that gave one *entrée* into the person—and what sets the frame for action emerges as powerfully exigent. Bettelheim insists that we must ask: what are the available fields for action? How does this field structure or delimit possibilities for human action? What emerges as central is the particular space for action and the sort of action that is possible, or nigh impossible, given the structure of that space.

We return to Rousseau's paradox. New ways of acting and being will be made possible by a transformed order. But how is such transformation of the action-field to take place unless changes in the self prompt or inspire such changed selves to alter their social institutions and practices? Perhaps we have tormented ourselves overlong by posing the question in this way. Perhaps instead we should assess alternative environments and the ways of being each seems to sustain or make possible. Perhaps we should think less in terms of the sovereign self and more in terms of linguistic universes and their constitutive terms.

A political vision treats the human being as *actus humanus* whose political being is realized through action together with others. This acting self takes on "political being" *given* his or her participation. But the therapeutic society spawns the self-obsessed self, not so much acting as reacting to every shift, however slight, in the internal climate. Although Freud would be implacably set against contemporary therapeutic culture as it has developed in our own society, he was a deconstructor of political being and identity. He aimed to give us other myths and truths and ways of thinking. But what got lost, or shunted to the side, was action. I now turn to a different side of the Freud coin, the question of psychoanalysis and representations of 'the female'.

Freud and the Rome Complex: *Mater Ecclesiae* Redux

Most often when Freud and women is the subject at hand the central questions concern Freud's three essays on female sexuality. But this ground has been traversed so many times, perhaps another tack is called for—not to supplant previous discussions but to turn away from penis envy to what may be a deeper set of issues.[24] I ask the reader to recall the discussion in Chapter 2, specifically Luther's insistence that Christianity must be Christocentric with devotion to the Mother shifted to the Son. As well, the institution Luther aimed to strip of all authority was symbolically female ("mater ecclescia"). One finds a fascinating analogy to Luther's project in Freud's life and work.

In a seminal essay, "Politics and Patricide in Freud's *Interpretation of Dreams*," Carl Schorske argues compellingly that psychoanalytic theory is in part a victory over politics, hence over the aspect of human affairs from which Freud had expected the most in youth. For the young Freud had political ambitions. He was, by background, conviction, and ethnicity a man of the left and the "new right" of his own day, virulently anti-Semitic, was for Freud a particular target. Nevertheless, Schorske argues, by the time we get to the Freud of his masterwork, *The Interpretation of Dreams*, we find a resolutely counter or anti-political thinker.

In a sense, the privatization and isolation forced upon Freud by his radical theories and his Jewish identity as the political winds in Austria shifted from relative liberalism to anti-Semitic reaction, helped to spawn an interiorizing of the subject. Freud interprets dreams in ways that neutralize politics "by reducing it to psychological categories...."[25] Throughout his work, Freud politicizes psychological categories (the dream-thought is censored by an inner censor not unlike the political writer being censored by those in authority, for example). But in so doing these categories—given the magesterial power of Freud's writings and their subsequent cultural impact—helped to legitimate political withdrawal, the Stoicism I noted above.

More interestingly with female symbolism in mind, is Freud's Rome neurosis. Freud himself tells the story. He became obsessed with Rome, with its topography and histories. In a four year period (1895–98), he traveled to Italy five times but never entered Rome. He recounts four Rome dreams: all themes of redemption and fulfillment unattained. He identifies Rome with "pleasure, rest, and cure; in short, an earthly city of recreation (re-creation), of resurrection," symbolically female. Freud's "forbidden Rome" represented many things, including a universal culture and a lost, great pagan past toward which Freud was ambivalent, his own childhood hero being Hannibal who nearly defeated Rome. "To take vengeance on the Romans" became for Freud a politicized filial project.

Rome as the object of desire, and Freud's resistance, speaks to Jewish-Catholic tension, discussed explicitly by Schorske and other critics and, less stressed by these same critics, to male identity and the seductive lure of 'the mother'.[26] Even as some of Freud's Jewish intellectual contemporaries turned to a baroque Catholic tradition, Freud, spurred by the increasing anti-Semitism of the 1890s, barred his own entry into Rome—"the Rome of pleasure, maternity, assimilation, fulfillment."[27] Political, religious, intellectual, oedipal, historical, and symbolic features are intermixed in Freud's Rome complex. But finally it is the Rome of 'Holy Mother" Freud ellides, making his peace with the pagan Rome that defeated his childhood hero, Hannibal.

Having resisted the lure of 'the mother', Freud finally entered Rome in 1921. The reader is advised not to misunderstand here: the point is not that Freud should have embraced a religious identity and made an explicit turn to *mater ecclesiae*. It would be arrogant and intemperate to suggest any such thing—particularly in light of the anti-Semitic currents in Freud's Catholic Vienna. Instead, the dimension I underscore with this brief sketch is Freud's elimination of the mother who promises re-creation from his own psychic constructions as well as his theory. He would symbolically 'kill' the father, as all men must, yet restore him. For the father embodies reality in a way the mother cannot: she, the baby at her breast, nourishes those dreams of utopian fulfillment Freud called "the oceanic feeling." Despite Freud's pretty thorough deconstruction of this utopian moment, later thinkers have turned to Freud's work, selectively, to write political rhapsodies. It is to a feminist utopianism, loosely connected to Freud as inspiration, that I next turn.

Putting Mother in Her Place

The text in question is Dorothy Dinnerstein's, *The Mermaid and the Minotaur*.[28] Hers is a feminized variant on the wider project of cultural, left-wing Freudianism of whom Norman O. Brown and Herbert Marcuse are the best-known representatives. She follows Marcuse's lead in translating several of Freud's key categories in such a way they become moldable into politically utopian evocations. Most importantly, Freud's *Ananke* or "necessity" becomes "scarcity"—a very different concept operating on another level entirely. For "scarcity," to those who presume it, can be overcome through more and more productivity.[29] "Necessity," however, is a return to the classical notion of built-in limiting conditions, unget-overables. We are finite. We shall die. Not just anything is possible. Life is filled with tragedy. And so on. The shift to "scarcity" does violence to Freud but serves the political purposes of thinkers in this genre well. That is the starting point. From that basis, with the human subject as a pre-posited ontological entity of a particular sort (*homo sexualis*), one can create what Michel Foucault calls "a new sexual evangelism in which the revelation of the truth, the stripping away of old hypocrisies, the promise of immediate fulfillment and future bliss are mingled together."[30]

Curiously, Dinnerstein's utopian project grants so much power to the overwhelming maternal figure she must be stripped of her force for society to change: the mother is both valorized and put in her place. Dinnerstein presumes that we are, as mother-reared humans, psychopathological in a present world she calls "diseased," "malignant," "poisoned," with motherhood itself described as "monstrous, atavistic." Our species-wide pathology is rooted in the oral stage, dominated by the mother-infant dyad, and the "project of sexual liberty" whereby we shall achieve "true spontaneity" and "full humanity" requires undoing things at this most basic level. Her argument turns on a complex notion of splitting I cannot detail here.[31] Most important for the purpose of this discussion is her insistence that the pre-verbal stage is *the* key to our collective psychopathology for that is where the psychic splits on which all else turns begin. Dinnerstein assumes a direct free-flow from orality to the totality of social structures, arrangements, and practices: this is the sort of psychologizing adaptations of Freud sometimes invite.

Let me explain. Dinnerstein observes correctly that ". . .the private and public sides of our sexual arrangements are not separable, and neither one is secondary to the other." She goes on to insist that *every* aspect of these arrangements is traceable to "a *single* childhood condition" and to claim that both our private and public arrangements "will *melt away* when that condition is abolished."[32] Dinnerstein accepts no *limits* on human freedom once we have ironed out the gender "asymmetry" that locates women preeminently as "mothers." (Remember the drastic redefinition—unacknowledged—of Freud's "necessity" on which this utopian moment turns.) But Dinnerstein's characterization of our current arrangements is so emotionally fraught and reductionist it offers no sense of a civic identity or polity. In her characterizations, the public world is reduced to the wholly defensive and destructive history-making of naughty boys and female private activity is treated in unflattering terms as well (though some good is buried there). History-making, public life, is described in such wholly negative ways one wonders if any good has ever come out of it and, more important, why any woman would want to get into it. Dinnerstein solves the latter problem by presuming that once women are free to be public beings on a par with men a revolution will already have occurred in any case.

By breaking the female monopoly of early child care, with men and women displaying homogeneous commitments to public and private life alike, we will reach, indeed we will inhabit, a new world. The pre-conditions for this world exist—and neither is political. One is "psychological," the other "technological." Political and economic structures and life are shrunk down to "technological" considerations. In this manner Dinnerstein's feminist utopia reflects, first, the depoliticization which is a constant temptation of Freudian approaches and, second, a society in which vital human issues are often reduced to technical problems amenable to technological solution. Surely the public conditions Dinnerstein alludes to are profoundly and inescapably political. But she has no way to handle these issues, having neither a political analysis of the present, nor a political vision of the future. Curiously from a feminist perspective, the *Mother*, symbolically represented as nurturant, re-creative, and currently assaulted *Nature*, is celebrated, but concrete mothers find the world's woes placed at their feet in the nursery. For mothers, unwittingly, serve as the agents behind the terrifying vision Dinnerstein unfolds as prelude to her utopian flight.[33]

At this juncture Freud's cautions and specified limits on what his—or any theory—can do serves as a helpful brake on promising too much from too little. He insisted that psychoanalysis could not serve to construct universal causal claims—claims that are inevitably culture-bound and blind. Freud's case histories retain their freshness and vitality because they are concrete evocations of the intrapsychic worlds of particular subjects.

One sign of the strength of Freud's accounts is that they allow for multiple interpretations. Appropriations of Freud that squeeze out space for interpretive pluralism by offering *the* explanation and *an* answer undercut features of psychoanalytic theory most instructive to the contemporary political theorist. The political implications of an interpretive as against a utopian evocation is that the interpretive thinker must take seriously the assent or dissent of human beings from social changes proposed or undertaken, ostensibly in their own behalf. Freud's expression of theoretical and therapeutic humility serves as a political object lesson despite the fact that his theory resolves politics into psychological categories.

Notes

1. Sigmund Freud, "The Question of a Weltanschauung" (Lecture 35), in *New Introductory Lectures on Psychoanalysis, Standard Edition*, vol. 22 (London: Hogarth, 1975), pp. 3–184, 158. Sigmund Freud was born in Freiberg, Moravia, 1856 and died in exile from Nazism in London in 1939.

2. Carl Schorschke, "Politics and Patricide in Freud's *Interpretation of Dreams*," in *Fin-de-siecle-Vienna* (New York: Knopf, 1980), pp. 181–207, 203.

3. Jerome S. Bruner, "Freud and the Image of Man," in *Freud and the Twentieth Century*, ed. Benjamin Nelson (Cleveland: World, 1957), pp. 277–86, 278.

4. I realize this is a controversial statement in light of feminist debate over Freud's theory of female psychology. But there is ample textual warrant for the claim that, in the most fundamental and important respects, Freud locates all human beings in pretty much the same fix.

5. See my introductory chapter for reminders of the debate over interpretation.

6. See my discussion of the female subject on pp. 303-12 in *Public Man, Private Woman* (Princeton: Princeton University Press, 1981) for a more complete treatment of the knowing female subject using psychoanalytic insights.

7. The similarities to Stoicism are striking. See Wolin's discussion in *Politics and Vision* (Boston: Little, Brown, 1960) pp. 78–82.

8. Who is the "we" here? I suppose it would have to be we heirs of a tradition of discourse that revolves around problematics of the one and the many, particular-universal, private-public.

9. Alarmed at the too ready acceptance of [a watered-down version of] psychoanalysis in America, Freud is quoted as saying: "They don't understand that I'm bringing them the plague." Cited in Sherry Turkle, *Psychoanalytic Politics* (New York: Basic Books, 1978), p. 4.

10. This community included men and women for women were involved, as equals, in psychoanalysis from the beginning. But it seems likely that Freud believed fewer women, as a percentage of the whole, could qualify for this company given his insistence that women—for a complex of reasons—are less capable of sublimation. See his discussion in *Civilization and its Discontents, Standard Edition*, vol. 21 (London: Hogarth, 1975), pp. 59–148, 103–4.

11. To Wolin this criticism does not go deeply enough and is only one of a number of even more serious shortcomings. See Wolin, *Politics and Vision*, p. 80.

12. See the discussion in Chapters 3 and 5 above as well as Michael Sandel, *Liberalism and the Limits of Justice* (Cambridge: Cambridge University Press, 1982) and Elshtain, *Public Man, Private Woman*, chap. 3.

13. Ironically, psychoanalysis can serve a critical wedge in authoritarian state socialist systems by asserting subjectivities, individualities, and pleasure against the grim and dreary productive ideology of those systems. But, as I argue below, subjectivity has become one of liberal society's most important products—not a threat but a major form of daily sustenance.

14. The reader is asked to recall the discussion of this freedom which loses the name of action in chap. 3 above.

15. See Sigmund Freud, *Group Psychology and the Analysis of Ego, Standard Edition*, vol. 18, (London: Hogarth, 1975), pp. 67–144.

16. This question figures explicitly in the discussion in Chapter 8 on war, political discourse, and female symbolism.

17. I will not here go over the extant literature on "the culture of narcissism," nor trace out the vagaries of our current immersion in a bewildering array of alternative routes to individual fulfillment or happiness.

I, and others, have had plenty to say on this elswhere. See, for example, Christopher Lasch, *The Culture of Narcissism* (New York: Warner Books, 1979) and Philip Rieff, *The Triumph of the Therapeutic* (New York: Harper Torchbook, 1968).

18. See my definition and discussion of a politics of displacement in *Public Man, Private Woman*, p. 91.

19. Richard Sennett, "Destructive Gemeinschaft," in *Beyond the Crisis* ed. Norman Birnbaum (New York: Oxford University Press, 1977), pp. 171–200, 176.

20. Ibid., p. 197.

21. Ibid., p. 177.

22. Bruno Bettelheim, *The Informed Heart* (New York: Avon, 1971) and Philip Hallie, *Lest Innocent Blood be Shed* (New York: Harper Colophon, 1979).

23. Bettelheim, *The Informed Heart*, p. 24.

24. Juliet Mitchell's *Psychoanalysis and Feminism* (New York: Pantheon, 1971) includes a detailed, lucid critique of feminist glosses on Freud's theory of female sexuality plus her own defense—one not without its own problems. See Elshtain, *Public Man, Private Woman*, pp. 275–84.

25. Schorske, "Politics and Patricide," p. 186. I will deal less with the oedipal configurations surrounding Freud, his father, and his father's death—one focus of Schorske's piece—and more on the so-called "Rome complex" where female imagery enters evocatively. For an alternative interpretation see Sebastiano Timpanaro, "Freud's Roman Phobia," *New Left Review*, no. 147 (Sept./Oct. 1984):4–31.

26. Schorske makes the most of the Catholic-Jewish question. See especially his footnote no. 26 with bibliographical data on Freud and this theme.

27. Schorske, p. 193.

28. Dorothy Dinnerstein, *The Mermaid and the Minotaur* (New York: Harper Colophon, 1977).

29. Of course, locating one's political hopes in the culture of productivity is less sustainable a thesis now that it was in the 1960s when Marcuse's vital works were most discussed.

30. Alan Sheridan, *Michel Foucault: The Will to Truth* (London: Tavistock, 1980), p. 68.

31. See Dinnerstein, p. 33. Also Sigmund Freud, "An Autobiographical Study," *Standard Edition*, vol. 20, (London: Hogarth, 1975), pp. 7–70, 30–31 and Jeffrey Lustman, "On Splitting," *The Psychoanalytic Study of the Child*, vol. 32 (1977), pp. 119–45, 119.

32. Dinnerstein, *Mermaid and Minotaur*, p. 159 (emphasis mine).

33. Dinnerstein's is but one of many current feminist appropriations of Freud. From a very different perspective, the object relations school, is Nancy Chodorow's influential, *The Reproduction of Mothering: Psychoanalysis and the Sociology of Gender* (Berkeley: University of California Press, 1978), though Chodorow, too, finds in exclusive mothering the causal context for social ills.

8

War and Political Discourse: From Machiavelli to Arendt

I am inclined to think that much of the present glorification of violence is caused by severe frustration of the faculty of action in the modern world.

Hannah Arendt

Meditating upon modern Western political thought, the contemporary analyst, particularly if she is sensitive to feminist questions and female-shaped concerns, is struck by the pervasive nexus forged between war and politics on the level of action and of thought. Because the very possibility of a future depends upon how this relationship plays itself out, I shall, in this final meditation, consider whether politics can be rescued from war.

Questions concerning war and thinking about war are often taken up in that sub-discipline of political science called "international relations." International relations, in turn, has long been dominated by a tradition of discourse called "realism." Two of the classic exemplars of realism—Niccolo Machiavelli and Thomas Hobbes—are inescapable architects of modern political thought. I shall look, first, at Machiavellian and Hobbesian constructions of political discourse in which violence and force are prime movers before turning to Hannah Arendt's *On Violence*, a text whose animating symbols and images suggests an alternative to the dominant theories of war in political thought.[1]

What Makes Realism Run

Realism's bracing promises are to spring politics free from the constraints of moral judgment and limitation, thereby assuring

103

its autonomy as historic force and discursive subject-matter, and to offer a picture of the world of men and states (women, too, I shall argue) as they really are rather than as we might yearn for them to be. Although there are antecedents, for example the Melian dialogue in Thucydides, Thrasymachus's contention that justice is the will of the stronger to Socrates in Plato's *Republic*, realism gets down to serious business with Machiavelli, moving on to theorists of sovereignty and apologists for *raison d'état* and culminating, in its early modern forms, with Hobbes's *Leviathan* before continuing the trek into the present. The contemporary realist locates himself inside a potent, well-honed tradition. Realist thinkers exude the confidence of those whose narrative long ago won the war. Realism's hegemony means that alternatives to realism are evaluated *from the standpoint of realism*, cast into a bin labeled "idealism" which, for the realist, is more or less synonymous with dangerous if well-intentioned naivete.

All twentieth-century students of politics are familiar with what realism presumes: a world of sovereign states, each seeking either to enhance or to secure its own power. State sovereignty is the motor that moves the realist system as well as its (nearly) immutable object. Struggle is endemic to the system and force is the court of last resort. It cannot be otherwise for states exist in a condition of anarchy in relation to one another. Wars will and must occur because there is nothing to prevent them. On one level, then, realism is a theory pitched to those structural imperatives that are said to bear on all actors in the international arena. No state, argues the realist, can reasonably or responsibly entertain the hope that through actions it takes, or refrains from taking, it may transform the wider context. Given that context, conflict is inevitable. Wars will and must occur simply because there is nothing to prevent them. The only logical solution to this unhappy state of affairs is a unitary international order to remedy international chaos.[2] Alas, what is logically unassailable may be practically unattainable given the realist refrain: a world of sovereign and suspicious states.

But realism, historically, is more: it involves a way of thinking (which I take up below); a set of presumptions about the human condition that secretes images of men and women and the parts they play in the human drama; and, as well, a potent rhetoric. Whether in its most uncompromising Hobbesian version or its less remorseless Machiavellian narrative, realism exaggerates certain features of the human condition and downgrades or ignores others. Interpreting realist texts from a vantage point informed by femi-

nist concerns, one is struck by the suppression and denial of female images and female-linked imperatives.

Thomas Hobbes, for example, describes a world of hostile
monads whose relations are dominated by fear, force, and instrumental calculation. Yet (and almost simple-mindedly), we
know this to be anthropologically false. From the simplest tribal
beginnings to the most complex social forms, women have had to
tend to infants—no matter what the men were up to—if life was to
go on in any sustained manner. That important features of the human condition are expunged from Hobbes's discursive universe, indicts his realism as an overdrawn distortion rather than the scientific depiction of the human condition at rock bottom he claimed
it to be.[3]

To be sure, the contemporary realist is unlikely to endorse a
full constellation of Hobbesian presumptions. He might reject Hobbes's vision of the state of nature, and his depiction of social relations, as dire and excessive. It is likely, however, that he will continue to affirm the wider conclusions Hobbes drew by analogy from
the miserable condition of human beings in the state of nature to
the unrelenting fears and suspicions of states in their relations to
one another. Yet is is plausible that if Hobbes omitted central features of human existence *internal* to civil societies and families
perhaps he is guilty of similar one-sidedness in his characterization of the world of states. To take up this latter possibility is to
treat Hobbes's realism as problematic, not paradigmatic.

Machiavelli goes down more smoothly in large part because we
have internalized so much of his legacy already. We all know the
story. Human beings are inconstant and trustworthy only in their
untrustworthiness. Political action cannot be judged by the standards of Christian morality. Civil virtue requires troops "well disciplined and trained" in time of peace in order to prepare for war:
this is a "necessity," a law of history.[4] '*Si vis pacem, para bel-
lum*," a lesson successive generations (or so the story goes) must
learn, though some, tragically, learn it too late; others in the nick
of time.

Machiavelli's narrative revolves around a public-private split
in and through which women are constituted, variously, as 'mir-
rors' to male war-making (a kind of civic cheerleader) or as a collective 'other', embodying the softer values and virtues out of place
within, and subversive of, *realpolitik*.[5] Immunized from political
action, the 'realist female' honors the gods and goddesses of the
household but she cannot embark on a project to bring her values
to bear on the civic life of her society. J. G. A. Pocock calls

Machiavelli's "militarization of citizenship" a potent legacy that subverts consideration of alternatives that do not bind civic and martial virtue together so tightly. Military preparedness, in this narrative, becomes the *sine qua non* of a viable polity. Though women cannot embody armed civic virtue, a task for the man, *vir*, they are sometimes drawn into the realist picture more sharply as occasions for war (we must fight to protect 'her'); as goads to action; as designated weepers over the tragedies war trails in its wake; or, in our own time, as male prototypes mobilized to meet dwindling manpower needs for the armed forces.[6] Rethinking realism using feminist questions forces us to see its central categories in a new light. The male *homme de guerre* retains his preeminent role, to be sure, but we recognize explicitly the ways in which his soldierly virilization is linked to the 'realist woman's' privatization.

Rescuing Politics from War: Arendt's 'Hope'

Hannah Arendt attempts to rescue politics from war, understanding that much has changed since the sixteenth and seventeenth centuries when the modern theory of realism was forged. For our problems lie not only in the compulsions of international relations, and dictated ways of viewing them, but in the order of modern, technological society. Dulled by the accretion of tropes and concepts that help us talk ourselves into war, situated inside a world of armed peace, Norman Mailer's claim in 1948 that "the ultimate purpose" of modern society is continuation of the army by other means seems prescient but not far-fetched.[7] Michael Foucault, too, argues that 'politics' (the single quotes are his) "has been conceived as a continuation, if not exactly and directly of war, at least of the military model as a fundamental means of preventing civil disorder. Politics . . . sought to implement the mechanism of the perfect army, of the disciplined mass, of the docile, useful troop . . ." and so on.[8]

In such an over-coordinated social world, the seduction of violence is an ever-present possibility, for violence promises a release from inner emptiness, a temporary escape from overplanned pointlessness. Paradoxically, the militarization of everyday life feeds rather than sates a deeper will to warfare as the prospect of escape from "impersonality, monotony, standardization," a chance to take and to share risks, to act rather than to persist in routinized motions.[9] That promise, however, is itself a victim of our armed peace. War technology devirilizes war fighting. The fighter exists for, and is eclipsed by, his weapons and that awesome arsenal, beyond his power to think coherently, of nuclear force.

On the level of discourse, one confronts a discourse of "disassociation" (my term) evident in contemporary "scientific" or "rationalist" realism. Such realists portray themselves as clearsighted, unsentimental analysts describing the world as it is. At present, hundreds of think tanks, universities, and government bureaucracies support the efforts of "scientifically minded brain trusters" who should be criticized, argues Arendt, not because they are thinking the unthinkable, rather because "they do not *think* at all."[10] The danger is this: a world of self-confirming theorems invites fantasies of control over events that we do not have. This contemporary 'scientization' of realism eclipses the strengths classical realists could claim, including awareness of the intractability of events and a recognition that relations between and among states are necessarily alienated ("foreign countries"). Hyperrationalized realism overfamiliarizes through abstracted models and logic, reducing states and their relations to models and simulative 'games'. Consider the following depiction of Western Europe by a strategic analyst: "Western Europe (like South Korea) amounts geographically to a peninsula projecting out from the Eurasian land mass from which large contingents of military force can emerge on relatively short notice to invade the peninsula."[11] Western Europe having been reduced to an undifferentiated, manageable piece of territory, it becomes (theoretically) expendable in the strategic plans that follow.

Modern thinkers of the abstracted unthinkable are not alone in doing violence to complex realities. "If truth is the main casualty in war, ambiguity is another," notes Paul Fussell, and one of the legacies of war is a "habit of simple distinction, simplification, and opposition."[12] Mobilized language, wartime's rhetoric of "binary deadlock," may persist and do much of our thinking for us. The absorption of politics by the language and imperatives of war becomes our permanent rhetorical condition. J. Glenn Gray reminds us that one basic task of a state at war is to portray the 'enemy' in terms as absolute and abstract as possible in order to distinguish as sharply as possible the act of killing from the act of murder. It is always "*the* enemy," a pseudo-concrete universal. This moral absolutism is constituted through language: there is no other way to do it. We are invited to hate without limit and told we are good citizens for doing so.

At one time war-fighting itself served, paradoxically, to deconstruct war rhetoric as soldiers rediscovered 'the concrete' in tragic

and terrifying ways. For example: Erich Maria Remarque's pro-
tagonist in *All Quiet on the Western Front* bayonets a frightened
French soldier who has leapt into the trench beside him in a panic,
seeking refuge. Four agonizing hours later the Frenchman dies and
when he has died, Remarque's hero, his capacity to perceive and
to judge concretely restored, speaks to the man he has killed:
"Comrade, I did not want to kill you. . . . But you were only an idea
to me before, an abstraction that lived in my mind and called forth
its appropriate response. It was that abstraction I stabbed."[13]
Gray, similarly, observes that the abstract bloodthirstiness expressed by civilians furthest removed from war-fighting was often
in contrast to the thinking of front-line soldiers whose moral absolutism frequently dissolved when they met 'the enemy' face to
face.[14] Because it is now possible for us to destroy 'the enemy'
without ever seeing him, abstract hatreds are less likely to rub
against concrete friction.

If realism's modern offspring invite dangerous disassociations,
an alternative discourse should be one less *available* for such purposes even as it offers a cogent orientation to systemic imperatives
in a world of sovereign and suspicious states. Too often alternatives
to 'thinking war' reproduce problematic features of the discourse
they oppose, for example, by insisting that we love (rather than
hate) abstract collectives. But 'the human race' is a pseudo-
concrete universal much like 'the enemy'. Pitched at a universal
level, anti-war discourse falls apart as one moves to specify connections between its inner vision and political exigency. Finally,
an alternative discourse must enable us to challenge war narratives with their traditional assurance of triumphant endings and
their prototypical figurations: fighting men, weeping women, even
as it acknowledges the attraction of the narrative and admits rather
than denies what Gray calls "the communal enthusiasm and ec-
stasies of war." Peace discourse that denies the violent undercur-
rents and possibilities in everyday life and in each one of us, perhaps by projecting that violence outward into others is but the
opposite side of the hard-line realist coin.

Hannah Arendt's *On Violence* responds to these concerns by
exposing our acceptance of politics as war by other means. What
are the historic transformations and discursive practices that made
possible the consensus Arendt notes "among political theorists
from Left to Right. . . that violence is nothing more than the most
flagrant manifestation of power"?[15] Her answer is multiple: strong
teleological visions of historic inevitability (known to us as "Progress"); the rise of theories of absolute power tied to the emergence

of the nation-state; the Old Testament tradition of "God's Commandments" which fed command-obedience conceptions of law in
Judaeo-Christian discourse; the infusion of biologism into political
discourse, particularly the notion that destruction is a law of nature, making violence a "life promoting force" through which men
purge the old and rotten—all these "time-honored opinions have
become dangerous." Locked into dangerously self-confirming ways
of thinking, we manage to convince ourselves that good comes out
of horrendous things; that somehow, in history, the end will justify
the means. Both classical liberals and their Marxist adversaries
share this discursive terrain, Arendt argues, though she is especially critical of "great trust in the dialectical 'power of negation'"
which soothes its adherents into believing that evil "is but a temporary manifestation of a still-hidden good."

Conflating the crude instrumentalism of violence with power,
the human ability to act in concert, to begin anew, guarantees further loss of space within which such empowerment is possible. In
this way violence nullifies power and stymies political being. One
important step away from the instrumentalism of violence and toward the possibility of a politics, then, is to resist the reduction of
politics to domination. Arendt evokes no image of isolated heroism
here; rather, she underscores the ways in which centralized orders
dry up power and political possibility. If we recognize the terms
through and the means by which this happens, we are less suscepti-
ble to unreflective mobilization. Arendt's discourse constitutes its
subjects as citizens: neither victims nor warriors. She paints no
rosy picture of her rescue effort.

Just as Gray argues that the will to war is deepened by the
emptiness of a false peace, Arendt believes that the greater a society's bureaucratization, the greater will be secret fantasies of destruction. Her repudiation of grandiose aims and claims—she does
not dictate what genuine politics should do or accomplish in-
strumentally for that would undermine her exposé of the teleolo-
gies on which violence and progress feed—is distilled from a great
boldness. For the symbolic alternative for political being she offers
is a plenary jolt (to the extent we see what she is doing and let it
work on us) to our reigning metaphors of the social contract, the
state of nature, leviathan, absolute sovereignty, totalized
bureacratization, and nationalistic triumphalism. Dominated by
this cluster of potent images, each of them suffused with violent
evocations or built on fears of violence, we face only more, and
deadlier, of what we've already got. Contrastingly, Arendt locates
as central a powerful but pacific image that evokes love, not war,

that offers *hope*, the human capacity that sustains political being.

Evidence of hopelessness is all around us. The majority of young people say they do not believe there will be a future of any sort. We shake our heads in dismay, failing to see that our social arrangements produce hopelessness and require it to hold themselves intact. But the possibility for hope is always present, rooted, ultimately, in "the fact of natality." Arendt's metaphor, elaborated most fully in the following passage from *The Human Condition*, is worth quoting in full: "The miracle that saves the world, the realm of human affairs, from its normal, 'natural' ruin is ultimately the fact of natality, in which the faculty of action is ontologically rooted. It is in otherwords, the birth of new human beings and the new beginning, the action they are capable of by being born. *Only the full experience of this capacity can bestow upon human affairs faith and hope, those two essential characteristics of human existence* . . . that found perhaps their most glorious and most succinct expression in the new words with which the Gospels announced their 'glad tiding': 'A Child has been born unto us.'"[16] The infant, like all beginnings, is vulnerable. We must nurture that beginning, not knowing and not being able to control the end of the story.

Arendt's evocation of natal imagery through its most dramatic historic narrative is not offered as an abstraction to be abstractly endorsed. Rather, she invites us to restore long-atrophied dispositions of commemoration and awe: birth, she declares, is a "miracle," a beginning that renews and irreversibly alters the world. Hers is a fragile yet haunting figuration that stirs recognition of our own vulnerable beginnings and our necessary dependency on others, on mother. Placed alongside this potent reality, political beginning construed as the actions of male hordes or contractualists seems parodic in large part because of the massive denial (of 'the female') on which it depends. A "full experience" of the "capacity" rooted in birth helps us to keep before our mind's eye the living reality of singularities, differences, individualities rather than a human mass as objects of possible control or manipulation toward ends dictated by others. By offering an alternative to collective violence and visions of triumph, Arendt politicizes by constituting her male and female objects as citizens who share alike the "faculty of action."[17]

But war is the central concern of this concluding chapter and Arendt's discourse must offer some specifiable orientation toward international relations.[18] Arendt's strategy shifts the ground on which we stand when we think about states and their relations. We become skeptical about the forms and the claims of the sovereign state; we deflate fantasies of control inspired by the reigning teleology of progress; we recognize the (phony) parity painted by a picture of equally sovereign states and are thereby alert to the many forms hegemony can take. Additionally, Arendt grants "forgiveness" a central political role as the only way to break remorseless cycles of vengeance and the repetition they invite. She embraces what might be called "ascesis," a refraining or withholding that allows refusal to bring all one's force to bear to surface as a strength, not a weakness.

Take the dilemma of the nuclear arms race which seems to have a life and dynamic of its own. An Arendtian perspective would see current arms control efforts for what they are—the arms race under another name negotiated by arms controllers, a bevy of experts with a vested interest in keeping the race alive so they can control it. On the other hand, her recognition of the limiting conditions internal to extant political orders prevents a leap into utopian fantasies of world order or total disarmament, the wholesale dismantling of defense along with deterrence. Neither of these options is particularly courageous—the first because it is a way of doing business as usual; the second because it lies outside the reach of possibility.

Instead, Arendt's perspective invites us—as a strong and dominant nation of awesome potential force—to take unilateral initiatives to break the cycle of vengeance and fear signified by our nuclear arsenals. Just as action from an individual, or group, disturbs the surface of everyday life, action from a single state may send shock waves that reverberate throughout the system. The war system is so deeply rooted that to begin to dismantle it in its current and highly dangerous form requires bold strokes.

At this juncture intimations of a alternative genealogy of political theory emerges: the Odyssey or homecoming, rather than the Iliad, or force as prototypical political myths; Socrates, Jesus of Nazareth, even Nietzsche in some of his teachings as articulators of the virtue of restraint and refusal to bring all one's power to bear. For it was Nietzsche, the most disillusioned of modern thinkers, who proclaimed the way out of armed peace—the only way—to be a people distinguished by their wars and victories who, from strength, "break the sword," thereby giving peace a chance. "Rather perish than hate and fear," he wrote, "and twice rather perish than make oneself hated and feared. . ."[19] As well, one can

identify an alternative political history, events, and movements
brought into being by men and women who embrace politics but
reject force.

To take up questions of war and political thought compels a
recognition of the powerful sway of received narratives, reminding
us that the concepts through which we think about war, peace,
and politics get repeated endlessly, shaping debates, constraining
consideration of alternatives, perhaps reassuring us that things
cannot really be much different than they are. As we nod an au-
tomatic "yes" when we hear the truism (though we may despair
of the truth it tells) that "there have always been wars," we simultaneously, if tacitly, acknowledge that "there have always been
war stories," for wars are deeded to us as texts.

We cannot identify "war itself" as an entity apart from a
powerful literary tradition that includes poems, epics, myths, official histories, first-person accounts, as well as the articulated theories I have discussed. War and the discourse of war are imbri-
cated, part and parcel of political reality. Contesting the terrain that
identifies and gives meaning to what we take these realities to be
does not mean one grants self-subsisting, unwarranted autonomy
to discourse; rather, it implies a recognition of the ways in which
received doctrines, war stories, may lull our critical faculties to
sleep, blinding us to possibilities that may lie within our reach.

Notes

1. Portions of this chapter are drawn from two different versions of
an essay, "Realism, Just War and Feminism in a Nuclear Age," *Political
Theory* 13 (February 1985): 39–57 and a second in Steven Lee and Av-
ner Cohen, eds., *Nuclear Weapons and the Future of Humanity* (Litt-
lefield, Adams, 1987).

2. Interestingly, Hannah Arendt, in *On Violence* (New York: Harcourt Brace Jovanovich, 1969), seems to endorse this view. Yet she quali-
fies it and, as I point out below, finally undermines the ground on which
this claim is raised.

3. Thomas Hobbes, *Leviathan*, ed. Michael Oakeshott (New York:
Collier Books, 1966), *passim*.

4. Niccolo Machiavelli, *The Prince and the Discourses* (New York:
Modern Library, 1950), p. 61.

5. Ibid., p. 503.

6. Nancy Huston, "Tales of War and Tears of Women," *Women's
Studies International Forum* 5 (Nos. 3/4, 1982): 271–82. Huston's essay
wonderfully evokes women's "supporting roles" in war narrative.

7. Cited in Paul Fussell, *The Great War and Modern Memory* (Oxford: Oxford University Press, 1975), p. 320.

8. Michel Foucault, *Discipline and Punish* (New York: Vintage Books, 1979), pp. 168–69.

9. J. Glenn Gray, *The Warriors: Reflections on Men in Battle* (New York: Harper Colophon, 1970), p. 224.

10. Arendt, *On Violence*, p. 12.

11. Cited in E. P. Thompson, *Beyond the Cold War* (New York: Pantheon, 1982), p. 10.

12. Fussell, *Great War and Modern Memory*, p. 79.

13. Erich Maria Remarque, *All Quiet on the Western Front* (New York: Fawcett, 1975), p. 195.

14. Gray, *The Warriors*, p. 135.

15. Arendt, *On Violence*, p. 35. The violence Arendt has in mind is that of groups or collectives, not individual outrage culminating in a single violent act: Melville's Billy Budd is her example.

16. Hannah Arendt, *The Human Condition* (Chicago: University of Chicago Press, 1958), p. 247.

17. Arendt, *On Violence*, p. 81.

18. Jonathan Schell, *The Fate of the Earth* (New York: Alfred A. Knopf, 1982) on pages 173–74 turns to Arendt's evocation of natal imagery to buttress his case against what he takes to be our collective race to nuclear extermination.

19. Gray, in *The Warriors*, cites in full the paragraph from Nietzsche's *The Wanderer and His Shadow* in which he repudiates the corruptions that flow from being hated and feared (pp. 225–60).

9

A Concluding Chapter That Doesn't

Posterity may know that we have not through silence permitted
things to pass away as in a dream.

Richard Hooker

An author sometimes feels obligated, having reached the conclusion of her text, to sum things up, to recall for the reader all that
has gone before. I shall resist this temptation since the reader is
certainly intelligent enough to do that. The dominant themes of
these meditations stand out clearly—concerns with the self, male
and female; with contrasting visions of politics and civic life; with
competing understandings of freedom, reason, equality, individualism, and so on. What might not emerge so clearly, though I hope
it does, is the sense of political urgency that resonates throughout
these meditations. Although I try to resist apocalyptic appeals and
convictions, I, with many others, often enough find myself peer-
ing over the edge of an abyss, wondering whether there shall be
a future.

To call the mind into play, to attempt, in Arendt's words, to
"think what we are doing," this is the task of political thought at
its best. Not being able to presume continuity in the affairs of men
and women, aware of the fragility of human events and our shared
vulnerability in light of current arsenals of potential force, we cannot predict. For prediction presumes regularity and requires
presumptions along the lines, "If x, then y." Yet the experience of
the past several generations cautions against any such ongoing
regularities. Assassinations, riots, technological breakthroughs,
cultural upheavals—all throw carefully constructed order, theoretical and actual, into disarray.

Yet we would locate ourselves somehow. Here political thought can help if we approach it with serious but playful intent, determined to try to place ourselves inside the world of the text knowing that the text is never the world. Understanding the text as a complex representation, the evocation of a world through words, we are ongoingly apprised of the power of words. Words matter. The words with which we characterize our daily lives and understand the lives of others matter. Whether we endorse Luther's "freedom of the Christian" or Rousseau's "civic freedom" makes a difference. Whether we hold that "equality" and "difference" are incompatible, and that we must therefore strive to attain some human "sameness" in order to promote social justice, or whether we believe in "equality *with* difference" locates us in the political world, and in a relation to our own identities, in quite diverse ways.

Perhaps we do not require political thought to tell us this. But few other forms of discourse have as their incessant preoccupations the terms of our individual and collective location in the world as unique 'ones' yet as a collective 'many'. American social identity, for example, is not only profoundly individual, it is also intensely linked to the belief that being an American means or ought to mean 'something'. Perhaps a guiding verse might be the New Testament image: the body is one but has many members. And, it should be noted, many voices. America has always promised a polyphonic chorus of diverse human voices, not the deadly monotone of the Nazi *Sprechor* in which all spoke as one, without exception. But this brings us directly up against Tocqueville's conundrum: our very freedom may convulse us, may corrode the possibility of many coming together as 'one' by fragmenting the many into irrevocably disassociated isolates. What glue can hold us together and help us to forge civic identities? How are we to restore any meaning to citizenship?

First, although we cannot re-create traditional forms of community, we can nurture community's living remnants—whether families, churches, neighborhoods, informal support groups, and associations. To do this we must get out of the house and into the world; we must resist powerful tugs toward privatization. Although women historically were defined as the preeminently private beings, the problem today goes much beyond (although it includes) the roles and identities of men and women. For modern consumerist societies push all of us toward the private pole, constituting us as takers and buyers rather than as givers and actors.

Second, and using powerful ideals from these meditations on

political thought, we can challenge the modern technocratic world-view with its reigning utilitarian ethic which dictates that nothing is of intrinsic value; hence, there are no intractable barriers to social engineering and experimentation. Given our only too human cravings for order in a world that seems out of control, and in light of the capacities of a technocratic world (at least, apparently) to satisfy these cravings, will our compulsion to control eventually take over the entire public sphere? Democracy is an unpredictable enterprise. Our patience with its ups and downs, its debates and compromises, indeed its very antiauthoritarianism, may wane as we become inured to more and more control—all in the name of freedom. Freedom from the vagaries of our bodies. Freedom from chance. Freedom from fear of the 'other'. But our engagement with political thought cautions that much can pass under the name freedom and it must be assayed critically rather than endorsed unthinkingly.

Third, all of us are in a position to reclaim, from our particular vantage points, the best in our tradition and democratic heritage, including our local practices of mutual *and* self-help. A popular bumper sticker one sees often nowadays is "Think Globally, Act Locally." This slogan enjoins us to consider the complex interdependencies of the modern world, to understand that what we do ramifies much beyond our own immediate sphere.[1] But it also acknowledges that we are not universal beings.[2] We exist in a particular time and place and we owe our greatest obligations to our hometown, with actions in its behalf radiating out to implicate us in larger purposes.

Sheldon Wolin claims that 'rejectionism' currently pervades our society—a form of rebellion evident when communities organize in the name of the common good against toxic waste, when tenants fight for rent control, whenever and wherever citizens come together to fight to preserve, to sustain, or to change a way of life. Knowing that community action will not change society *in toto*, one nevertheless acts *from* but not simply *for* the self. Many feminist groups take precisely this communal, de-centralized form, working on health collectives, battered women shelters, support groups for handicapped women or single mothers—the list goes on. Through such acts of citizenship, individuals are transformed and, as well, the frightening political drain upward, reposing more and more power in centralized, sovereign states—and corporations—is at least partially stemmed. This is a reasonable hope. And hope, as Arendt insists, is the root of action.

Notes

1. Recall, for a moment, the discussion in Chapter 4 concerning the effects of our meat-eating habits on protein availability in much of the rest of the world.

2. See Michael Walzer, *Spheres of Justice* (New York: Basic Book, 1983), for a discussion of our multiple understandings of social *goods* in diverse spheres.

Bibliography

Addams, Jane. *Democracy and Social Ethics*. New York: Macmillan, 1902.

———. *Forty Years at Hull House*. [Being *Twenty Years at Hull House* and *The Second Twenty Years at Hull House* in one vol.] New York: Macmillan, 1935.

———. *The Long Road of Woman's Memory*. New York: Macmillan, 1916

———. *Newer Ideals of Peace*. London: Macmillan, 1907.

———. *Peace and Bread in Time of War*. Boston: G. K. Hall, 1960.

———. *Twenty Years at Hull House*. New York: Macmillan, 1968.

Arendt, Hannah. *Eichmann in Jerusalem*. New York: Penguin Books, 1963.

———. *The Human Condition*. Chicago: University of Chicago Press, 1958.

———. *On Revolution*. New York: Penguin Books, 1972.

———. *On Violence*. New York: Harcourt Brace Jovanovich, 1969..

Atkinson, Ti-Grace. "Theories of Radical Feminism." In *Notes from the Second Year*, edited by Shulamith Firestone. (N.p., 1970).

Avineri, Shlomo. *Hegel's Theory of the Modern State*. Cambridge: Cambridge University Press, 1974.

Barker-Benfield, G. J. " 'Mother Emancipator': The Meaning of Jane Addams' Sickness and Cure," *Journal of Family History* (Winter 1979):395–420.

Berry, Wendell. *The Unsettling of America: Culture and Agriculture*. New York: Avon, 1977.'

Bettelheim, Bruno. *The Informed Heart*. New York: Avon, 1971.

Blum, Lawrence A. "Kant's and Hegel's Moral Rationalism: A Feminist Perspective," *Canadian Journal of Philosophy* 12 (June, 1982):287–302.

Bourne, Randolph. *The Radical Will: 1911–1918*. New York: Urizen, 1978.

Brownmiller, Susan. *Against Our Will: Men, Women and Rape*. New York: Simon and Schuster, 1975.

Bruner, Jerome S. "Freud and the Image of Man." In *Freud and the Twentieth Century*, edited by Benjamin Nelson, pp. 277–86. Cleveland: World, 1957.

Cassirer, Ernst. *The Question of Jean-Jacques Rousseau*. Translated by Peter Gay. Bloomington, Ind.: Indiana University Press, 1967.

Chodorow, Nancy. *The Reproduction of Mothering: Psychoanalysis and the Sociology of Gender*. Berkeley: University of California Press, 1978.

Daly, Mary. *Gyn/Ecology: The Metaethics of Radical Feminism*. Boston: Beacon Press, 1979.

Darnton, Robert. "The Origins of Modern Reading," *The New Republic*, Feb. 27, 1984, pp. 26–33.

Davis, Allen F. *American Heroine: The Life and Legend of Jane Addams*. New York: Oxford University Press, 1973.

Davis, Natalie Zemon. "Men, Women and Violence: Some Reflections on Equality," *Smith Alumnae Quarterly* (April 1972):12–15.

Dinnerstein, Dorothy. *The Mermaid and the Minotaur*. New York: Harper Colophon, 1977.

Dronke, Peter, ed. *Women Writers of the Middle Ages*. Cambridge: Cambridge University Press, 1984.

Duncan, Graeme. *Marx and Mill: Two Views of Social Conflict and Social Harmony*. Cambridge: Cambridge University Press, 1973.

Dyson, Freeman. *Weapons and Hope*. New York: Basic Books, 1984.

Elshtain, Jean Bethke. "Antigone's Daughters," *Democracy* (April 1982):46–59.

———. "Kant, Politics and Persons: The Implications of His Moral Philosophy," *Polity* 14 (Winter 1981):205–21.

———. *Public Man, Private Women: Women in Social and Political Thought*. Princeton: Princeton University Press, 1981.

———. "Toward a Reflective Feminist Theory," *Women and Politics* 3 (Winter 1983):7–26.

———. "Woman as Mirror and Other," *Humanities in Society* 5 (Winter/Spring 1982):29–44.

Enloe, Cynthia. *Does Khaki Become YOU? The Militarisation of Women's Lives*. London: Pluto Press, 1983.

Erikson, Erik. *Young Man Luther*. New York: W. W. Norton, 1958.

Foucault, Michel. *Discipline and Punish*. New York: Vintage, 1979.

Freud, Sigmund. "An Autobiographical Study." In *The Complete Psychological Works of Sigmund Freud*, 24 vols. London: Hogarth, 1975. (Hereafter called *Standard Edition*), vol. 20, 7–70.

——. "Civilization and its Discontents," *Standard Edition*, vol. 21, pp. 59–148.

——. "Group Psychology and the Analysis of Ego." *Standard Edition*, vol. 18, pp. 67–144.

——. "The Question of a Weltanschauung." *New Introductory Lectures on Psychoanalysis, Standard Edition*, vol. 22, pp. 3–184.

Fussell, Paul, *The Great War and Modern Memory*. Oxford: Oxford University Press, 1975.

Geertz, Clifford. *The Interpretation of Cultures*. New York: Basic Books, 1973.

Gilligan, Carol. *In a Different Voice*. Cambridge, Mass.: Harvard University Press, 1982.

Gilman, Charlotte Perkins. *Women and Economics*. New York: Harper Torchbook, 1966.

Gray, J. Glenn. *The Warriors: Reflections on Men in Battle*. New York: Harper Colophon, 1970.

Gregor, Mary J. *Laws of Freedom*. Oxford: Basil Blackwell, 1963.

Hallie, Philip. *Lest Innocent Blood Be Shed*. New York: Harper Colophon, 1979.

Hegel, G. W. F. *Phenomenology of Spirit*. Translated by A. V. Miller. London: Oxford University Press, 1977.

——. *Philosophy of Right*. Translated by T. M. Knox. London: Oxford University Press, 1967.

Hobbes, Thomas. *The Leviathan*. Edited by Michael Oakeshott. New York: Collier Books, 1966.

Huizinga, Johan. *The Waning of the Middle Ages*. Garden City, N.Y.: Doubleday, 1954.

Huston, Nancy. "Tales of War and Tears of Women," *Women's Studies International Forum*, vol. 5, no. 3/4 (1982):271–82.

John Paul II. "On Pilgrimage: The UN Address." *Origins*, vol. 9, no. 42 (1979):675–80.

Jordanova, L. J. "Natural Facts: A Historical Perspective on Science and Sexuality." In *Nature, Culture and Gender*, edited by Carol P. MacCormack and Marilyn Strathern, pp. 42–69. Cambridge: Cambridge University Press, 1980.

Kant, Immanuel. *Critique of Pure Reason*. Translated by Norman Kemp Smith. New York: The Modern Library, 1958.

———. *Groundwork of the Metaphysic of Morals*. Translated by H. J. Paton. New York: Harper Torchbook, 1964.

———. *The Metaphysical Elements of Justice*. Indianapolis: Bobbs-Merrill, 1965.

———. *On the Old Saw: That May be Right in Theory But It Won't Work in Practice*. Philadelphia: University of Pennsylvania Press, 1974.

Kraditor, Aileen S. *Up From the Pedestal. Writings in the History of American Feminism*. Chicago: Quadrangle Books, 1968.

Lasch, Christopher. *The Culture of Narcissism*. New York: Warner Books, 1979.

———. *The New Radicalism in America*. New York: Vintage, 1965.

———, ed. *The Social Thought of Jane Addams*. Indianapolis: Bobbs-Merrill, 1965.

Leach, William. *True Love and Perfect Union: The Feminist Reform of Sex and Society*. New York: Basic Books, 1980.

Locke, John. *Two Treatises of Government*. Edited by Peter Laslett. New York: New American Library, 1965.

Lustman, Jeffrey. "On Splitting." *The Psychoanalytic Study of the Child* 32 (1977):119–45.

Luther, Martin. *Three Treatises*. N.p.: Fortress Press, 1960.

Machiavelli, Niccolo. *The Prince and the Discourses*. New York: Modern Library, 1950.

Macpherson, C. B. *The Political Theory of Possessive Individualism*. Oxford: Oxford University Press, 1963.

Magee, Bryan, ed. *Modern British Philosophy*. New York: St. Martin's Press, 1971.

McManners, John. *Death and the Enlightenment*. Oxford: Clarendon Press, 1981.

McMillan, Carol. *Women, Reason and Nature*. Oxford: Basil Blackwell, 1982.

Mead, George Herbert. *Mind, Self and Society*. Chicago: University of Chicago Press, 1962.

Mill, John Stuart. *On the Subjection of Women*. Greenwich, Conn.: Fawcett, 1973.

Miller, James. *Rousseau: Dreamer of Democracy*. New Haven: Yale University Press, 1984.

Mitchell, Juliet. *Psychoanalysis and Feminism*. New York: Pantheon, 1971.

O'Faolain, Julia, and Lauro Martines, eds. *Not in God's Image*. New York: Harper Torchbook, 1973.

Okin, Susan Moller. *Women in Western Political Thought*. Princeton: Princeton University Press, 1978.

O'Neill, William. *Everyone Was Brave: The Rise and Fall of Feminism in America*. Chicago: Quadrangle Books, 1969.

Paolucci, Henry, ed. *The Political Writings of St. Augustine*. Chicago: Henry Regnery, 1967.

Remarque, Erich Maria. *All Quiet on the Western Front*. New York: Fawcett, 1975.

Rieff, Philip. *The Triumph of the Therapeutic*. New York: Harper Torchbook, 1968.

Rousseau, Jean-Jacques. *The Confessions*. Translated by J. N. Cohen. Baltimore: Penguin Books, 1954.

———. *Emile*. Translated by Allan Bloom. New York: Basic Books, 1979.

———. *The First and Second Discourses*. Translated by Roger and Judith Masters. New York: St. Martin's Press, 1964.

———. *The Government of Poland*. Translated by Wilmoore Kendall. Indianapolis: Bobbs-Merrill, 1972.

———. *On the Origin of Language*. Translated by J. Moran and A. Gode. New York: Frederick Unger, 1966.

———. *On the Social Contract, with Geneva Manuscript and Political Economy*. Translated by Judith Masters. New York: St. Martin's Press, 1978.

Ruddick, Sara. "Maternal Thinking." In *Mothering: Essays in Feminist Theory*, ed. Joyce Trebilcot, pp. 213–300. Totowa, N.J.: Rowman and Allanheld, 1984.

Rupp, E. G., and Benjamin Drewery. *Martin Luther*. London: Edward Arnold, 1970.

Sanday, Peggy Reeves. *Female Power and Male Dominance*. Cambridge: Cambridge University Press, 1981.

Sandel, Michael J. *Liberalism and the Limits of Justice*. Cambridge: Cambridge University Press, 1982.

Schorske, Carl. "Politics and Patricide in Freud's *Interpretation of Dreams*." In *Fin-de-siecle Vienna*. New York: Knopf, 1980.

Schwartz, Joel. *The Sexual Politics of Jean-Jacques Rousseau*. Chicago: University of Chicago Press, 1984.

Sennett, Richard. "Destructive Gemeinschaft." In *Beyond the Crisis*, edited by Norman Birnbaum. New York: Oxford University Press, 1977.

Sheridan, Alan. *Michel Foucault: The Will to Truth*. London: Tavistock, 1980.

Smith, Rogers. " 'One United People': Discriminatory Citizenship Laws and the American Quest for Community, 1800–1937." Yale University ms., 1983.

Smith-Rosenberg, Carroll. "Beauty, the Beast, and the Militant Woman." In *A Heritage of Her Own*, edited by Nancy F. Cott and Elizabeth H. Pleck, pp. 197–221. New York: Touchstone Book, 1979.

Stanton, Elizabeth Cady, Susan B. Anthony, and Matilda Joslyn Gage, eds. *History of Woman Suffrage*, vol. 1. Rochester, N.Y.: Charles Mann, 1881.

———. *History of Woman Suffrage*, vol. 2. Rochester, N.Y.: Charles Mann, 1886.

Stanton, Elizabeth Cady. *Eighty Years and More: Reminiscences 1814–1897*. New York: Schocken Books, 1971.

———. *Solitude of Self*. Kailua, Hawaii: published privately by Doris M. Ladd and Jane Wilkins Pultz, 1979.

Tanner, Tony. "Julie and 'La Maison Paternelle': Another Look at Rousseau's *La Nouvelle Heloise*." In *The Family in Political Thought*, edited by Jean Bethke Elshtain, pp. 96–124. Amherst, Mass.: University of Massachusetts Press, 1982.

Taylor, Barbara. *Eve and the New Jerusalem*. New York: Pantheon, 1983.

Taylor, Charles. "Atomism." In *Power, Possessions and Freedom: Essays in Honor of C. B. Macpherson*, edited by Alkis Kantos, pp. 39–61. Toronto: University of Toronto Press, 1979.

———. "What's Wrong with Negative Liberty?" In *Essays in Honour of Isaiah Berlin*, pp. 176–93. Oxford: Oxford University Press, 1980.

Thompson, E. P. *Beyond the Cold War*. New York: Pantheon, 1982.

Thompson, W. D. J. Cargill. "Martin Luther and the 'Two Kingdoms'." In *Political Ideas*, edited by David Thomson. New York: Penguin, 1982.

Tocqueville, Alexis de. *Democracy in America*, ed. Phillips Bradley. New York: Vintage, 1945.

Todd, John M. *Luther: A Life*. New York: Crossroad, 1982.

Troeltsch, Ernst. *The Social Teachings of the Christian Churches*. Translated by Olive Wyon, vol. 2. Chicago: University of Chicago Press, 1981.

Tronto, Joan. "The Scottish Enlightenment, Contextual Morality and Current Feminist Debate." Unpub. ms., 1984.

Turkle, Sherry. *Psychoanalytic Politics*. New York: Basic Books, 1978.

United States Catholic Bishops Pastoral Letter on War and Peace. *Origins*, May 19, 1983, pp. 1–32.

Wade, Mason, ed. *The Writings of Margaret Fuller*. New York: Viking Press, 1941.

Walzer, Michael. *Just and Unjust Wars*. New York: Basic Books, 1979.

——. *Spheres of Justice*. New York: Basic Books, 1983.

Whitbeck, Caroline. "The Maternal Instinct." In *Mothering: Essays in Feminist Theory*, edited by Joyce Trebilcot, pp. 185–92. Totowa, New Jersey: Rowman and Allanheld, 1984.

Williams, Bernard. "Conflicts over Values," in *Moral Luck*. Cambridge: Cambridge University Press, 1981.

Wilson, Katharine M. *Medieval Woman Writers*. Athens, Georgia: University of Georgia Press, 1984.

Wolin, Sheldon. *Politics and Vision*. Boston: Little, Brown, 1960.

Wollstonecraft, Mary. *A Vindication of the Rights of Woman*. New York: W. W. Norton, 1967.

Zahn, Gordon. *Another Part of the War: The Camp Simon Story*. Amherst, Mass.: University of Massachusetts Press, 1979.

Index